THE NICARAGUAN REVOLUTION

Gary E. McCuen

IDEAS IN CONFLICT SERIES

publications inc.

411 Mallalieu Drive
Hudson, Wisconsin 54016

Illustration & photo credits
Vsevolod Arsenyev 169, Barricada/Roger 139, Harriet R. Blood 18, Brookins 119, DeOre 54, 115, Gorbarukov 54, Gorrell 67, The Guardian 158, Susan Harlan 103, Ollie Harrington 59, Charles Keller 75, 109, The Militant 136, Bernard Nietschmann 92, Ann Roetzel 11, 31, Sanders 146, David Seavey 45, 177, Trever 125, U.S. Department of State 38, 130, 151, Wells 138, Wright 85.

© 1986 by Gary E. McCuen Publications, Inc.
411 Mallalieu Drive • Hudson, Wisconsin 54016
  (715) 386-5662
International Standard Book Number 0-86596-058-5
Printed in the United States of America

CONTENTS

CHAPTER 4   THE SANDINISTAS AND U.S. POLICY

CHAPTER 5   NICARAGUA: A THREAT TO OUR
            SECURITY?

REASONING SKILL DEVELOPMENT

These activities may be used as individualized study guides
for students in libraries and resource centers or as discussion
catalysts in small group and classroom discussions.

IDEAS in CONFLICT®

This series features ideas in conflict on political, social and moral issues. It presents counterpoints, debates, opinions, commentary and analysis for use in libraries and classrooms. Each title in the series uses one or more of the following basic elements:

Introductions that present an issue overview giving historic background and/or a description of the controversy.

Counterpoints and debates carefully chosen from publications, books, and position papers on the political right and left to help librarians and teachers respond to requests that treatment of public issues be fair and balanced.

Symposiums and forums that go beyond debates that can polarize and oversimplify. These present commentary from across the political spectrum that reflect how complex issues attract many shades of opinion.

A global emphasis with foreign perspectives and surveys on various moral questions and political issues that will help readers to place subject matter in a less culture-bound and ethno-centric frame of reference. In an ever shrinking and interdependent world, understanding and cooperation are essential. Many issues are global in nature and can be effectively dealt with only by common efforts and international understanding.

Reasoning skill study guides and discussion activities provide ready made tools for helping with critical reading and evaluation of content. The guides and activities deal with one or more of the following:

RECOGNIZING AUTHOR'S POINT OF VIEW

INTERPRETING EDITORIAL CARTOONS

VALUES IN CONFLICT

WHAT IS EDITORIAL BIAS?

6

WHAT IS SEX BIAS?
WHAT IS POLITICAL BIAS?
WHAT IS ETHNOCENTRIC BIAS?
WHAT IS RACE BIAS?
WHAT IS RELIGIOUS BIAS?

*From across **the political spectrum** varied sources are presented for research projects and classroom discussions. Diverse opinions in the series come from magazines, newspapers, syndicated columnists, books, political speeches, foreign nations, and position papers by corporations and non-profit institutions.*

About the Editor

Gary E. McCuen is an editor and publisher of anthologies for public libraries and curriculum materials for schools. Over the past 16 years his publications of over 200 titles have specialized in social, moral and political conflict. They include books, pamphlets, cassettes, tabloids, filmstrips and simulation games, many of them designed from his curriculums during 11 years of teaching junior and senior high school social studies. At present he is the editor and publisher of the *Ideas in Conflict* series and the *Editorial Forum* series.

FROM SANDINO TO SOMOZA

James D. Rudolph and Richard L. Millett

With the exception of a brief nine-month period in 1925-26, the United States maintained troops in Nicaragua from 1912 until 1933. Over 2,700 sailors and marines had taken part in the 1912 intervention. Most were quickly withdrawn, but a legation guard of at least 100 men was retained in Managua until 1925 as a symbol of United States determination not to allow revolutionary change. As a result the Conservatives, who were almost certainly the minority party, managed to remain in power until 1925.

During this period Nicaragua remained poor, under-developed, and thinly populated. In 1914 the total population was only 703,540, the bulk of which was engaged in subsistence agriculture. Coffee, much of it from foreign-owned properties in the Matagalpa area, was the major export. Small amounts of gold and bananas were also exported. Except for frequent loans to the government, foreign investments were small. Nicaragua's principal asset in the eyes of the rest of the world remained its location as a potential canal site.

Since the canal through Panama was about to open, the United States had no interest in constructing a Nicaraguan canal—but it was interested in making sure that no other nation did so. . .

Nicaragua: A Country Study, 1981, edited by James D. Rudolph, published by U.S. Government Printing Office for Department of the Army.

The Revolt of Augusto Cesar Sandino

On July 1, 1927, Sandino issued his first political manifesto, denouncing President Moncada as a traitor, vowing to drive the Americans out of Nicaragua, and calling for joint Latin American construction of a Nicaraguan canal. Fifteen days later he attacked the small marine garrison in the mountain town of Ocotal. The attack was repulsed; heavy losses were incurred, but Sandino regrouped his forces and began a guerrilla campaign that would last until 1933.

Sandino's dogged resistance continually frustrated marine efforts to restore stability and turn over internal security functions to the National Guard. The guerrilla leader was never able to capture and hold a major town, nor could his forces seriously threaten the government in Managua. But his efforts did point up the government's dependence on United States support as well as increase opposition to the intervention within Latin America and the United States. Sandino was absent from Nicaragua from June 1929 to May 1930, traveling to Mexico in the vain hope of receiving support from that nation, but his lieutenants carried on the fight. For the marines this ongoing campaign became a source of endless frustrations. Massive sweeps proved ineffective, and aggressive small unit patrols, while effective, were costly and exhausting. Increasingly the United States sought to turn over combat operations to Nicaragua's National Guard and place marine units in a reserve role in major cities. . .

The Somoza Dynasty, 1933-77
The Establishment of the Dynasty

The final task of the intervention was to turn over command of the National Guard to Nicaraguan officers. Enough junior officers had been trained by the marines to fill those positions, but selecting senior commanders proved more difficult. An agreement was reached between the two parties to divide most of these posts equally, but the top position of *jefe director* of the Guard remained in dispute. The final decision was that the choice would be made by the victor in the 1932 election, with the approval of the United States and Moncada. After some hesitation Anastasio Somoza Garcia was selected by President-elect Sacasa. . .

Final withdrawal of the marines took place immediately following the January 1, 1933, inauguration of Sacasa as president. The new government inherited severe financial problems, but even more threatening was the continuing operation of Sandino. His long resistance to the American intervention had won him considerable stature throughout Latin America. As a result both the United States and the Moncada administration had been the object of strong criticism, while a torrent of writings had glorified Sandino. Domestic support, international prestige, and budgetary necessity all made some sort of arrangement with the guerrilla leader imperative.

Fortunately for the new president, Sandino quickly made it clear that he intended to honor his pledge to cease fighting once the marines were withdrawn. Preliminary negotiations had begun in December 1932, but final agreement did not come until February 2, 1933. The government offered a general amnesty, land, and jobs in northern Nicaragua for Sandino's followers, and permission for him to maintain a personal guard of 100 armed men. The National Guard was unhappy with the agreement—especially the last provision—and their dissatisfaction grew when they became convinced that Sandino turned over only a fraction of his arms to the government. Internal divisions and lack of funds, however, gave them little alternative other than to accept the pact.

The pact with Sandino ended the fighting but did not restore political harmony to Nicaragua. The Guard's antagonism towards Sandino and his followers was increased when the Nicaraguan Congress voted a substantial monthly sum to pay for Sandino's personal guard and shortly thereafter passed another bill reducing military salaries. The conservatives were angered by Somoza's efforts to remove Conservative officers from the National Guard and replace them with individuals loyal to him personally. Sandino became increasingly hostile toward the Guard, especially after an August clash which left five of his followers dead. The president was fearful of Sandino's political ambitions and repeatedly pressured him not to form his own political party as he had intended. The various conflicts finally came to a head in early 1934.

Ann Roetzel

Nicaragua: A Country Study, 1981, edited by James D. Rudolph, published by U.S. Government Printing Office for Department of the Army.

Sandino's survival represented a major obstacle to Somoza's presidential ambitions and to the status of the Guard, which Sandino repeatedly denounced as unconstitutional. In January, at a meeting of high-ranking officers, the decision was made to eliminate the guerrilla leader. Sacasa was not informed of these plans, but the *jefe director* did try to obtain the approval of the United States minister, Arthur Bliss Lane, for Sandino's arrest. Lane refused to go along with these plans, fearing that such action would renew civil conflict in Nicaragua. Despite this rebuff the Guard remained determined to eliminate Sandino. Sacasa was not involved in the plot, but he was nervous about the growing tension and the guerrillas' refusal to give up any of their arms. He invited Sandino to a February 1934 conference with him in Managua. After several meetings, some of the issues were apparently resolved, but as Sandino and his chief aides were leaving a farewell dinner at the presidential palace on February 21 they were seized by a Guard contingent acting under Somoza's orders, taken to the airfield, executed, and secretly buried. At the same time another force attacked Sandino's followers along the Rio Coco and largely destroyed them. A few led by Pedro Altamirano, escaped and carried on a limited guerrilla campaign until Altamirano was killed in 1937; but Sandino's immediate threat to Somoza and the Guard was removed by the February 1934 actions. . .

Social Conditions under the Somoza Family Dictatorships

From the time of its independence from Spanish colonial rule in the early nineteenth century, Nicaragua had been ruled by and for a socioeconomic elite consisting of, perhaps, 5 percent of the population. Under Anastasio Somoza Debayle, the third Somoza family ruler, the size of the elite was further constricted. Using family inheritances and business dealings made possible by his dictatorial control of the government apparatus, Somoza accumulated a fortune worth hundreds of millions of dollars. By the mid-1970s as much as one-quarter of Nicaragua's total assets were owned by Somoza. In the process of amassing this fortune, however, the dictator alienated the jealous traditional elite; in the days preceding his fall from power a popular Nicaraguan joke held that Somoza had 15,003 supporters: the 15,000-member National Guard, his wife, son, and mistress.

Nicaragua had witnessed little in the way of mass-based political movements before the 1970s. For a decade in the late 1920s and early 1930s General Augusto Cesar Sandino and several hundred rebels had waged a guerrilla campaign against the government and a contingent of United States Marines that occupied the country. Then in 1961 a small guerrilla organization—the FSLN—was founded, taking its name from the general who had been murdered by the first President Somoza and his fledgling National Guard in 1934. . .

The FSLN Victory in 1979

Before the FSLN victory the benefits of Nicaragua's substantial growth had accrued to only a small portion of the population. In 1977 the wealthiest 5 percent of the population earned about 28 percent of total income; the poorest 50 percent earned only about 12 percent of the total. A skewed income distribution between rural and urban areas also existed. In 1972 the average income in Managua was three and one-half times higher than that in the rural areas. The average income of Managua's families in the lower 50 percent income bracket was more than 5.5 times higher than that of the corresponding rural group. But within the rural group there was a higher concentration of income; the wealthiest 5 percent of Nicaragua's farmers earned 42 percent of total rural income compared to 27 percent for the corresponding urban group. . .

The struggle against Somoza was not strictly a class-based revolution; virtually all sectors of Nicaraguan society had joined in the effort to oust the dictator. In 1978 and 1979 a sizable portion of poor and working-class Nicaraguans were organized, in their neighborhoods and workplaces, into militias and various other organizations that supported the struggle spearheaded by the FSLN guerrilla units. Businessmen, professionals, the Roman Catholic Church, and the traditionally compliant opposition political parties also cooperated with the Sandinistas and led the successful effort to rally international opinion behind the effort to oust Somoza.

Internationally isolated and facing military defeat on five different fronts throughout the country, Somoza fled Nicaragua on July 17, 1979. Within twenty-four hours the National Guard had disintegrated, and the FSLN victory was assured. The guerrilla commanders triumphantly entered Managua and set up the Government of National Reconstruction amid a tremendous groundswell of domestic and international goodwill. But the new government was aptly named—for the victory had come at a high cost: The economy had been devastated: commerce and agriculture were almost completely disrupted, and damage inflicted to industrial plant alone was estimated at U.S. $50 million. . .

The Somozas left the nation with over U.S. $1.5 billion in debts and only some U.S. $3.5 million in international reserves. Oddly enough coffee production had risen in 1979, but production of every other major crop had dropped. Cotton production was only 70 percent of the 1978 level, grain production was off by 20 percent, and livestock declined by 20 percent. Capital expenditures during 1979 fell by 36 percent, and the GDP declined by 25.8 percent.

Human and material losses from the conflict were staggering. An estimated 30,000 to 50,000 Nicaraguans had been killed during the civil conflict, a figure equal to about 1 percent of the population, and some 100,000 had been injured. An estimated 150,000 persons had been left homeless. Approximately 150,000 had fled to Honduras or Costa Rica during the war, and many more had become internal refugees. Destruction of the industrial base represented 23 percent of its total value, and losses to commercial establishments from fighting and looting represented 34 percent of their total value. Total material costs, including physical damage, loss of production, and capital flight probably exceeded U.S. $1.5 billion. Large-scale international relief efforts prevented the danger of starvation and averted immediate economic collapse, but the task of economic reconstruction was nonetheless overwhelming.

CHAPTER 2

SANDINISTA SOCIAL REFORMS:
IDEAS IN CONFLICT

2 PROPONENTS' FORUM

GIVE CHANGE A CHANCE

Institute for Food and Development Policy

The Institute for Food and Development Policy is a non-profit research and educational center that deals with the problems and causes of hunger on a global basis. The center publishes books, newsletters and educational curriculums.

Points to Consider

1. Why does foreign aid fail to end hunger?
2. What is the difference between a revolution and a coup?
3. How is life described under the Somoza dictatorship in Nicaragua?
4. What changes have been made by the Sandinistas?
5. How is U.S. policy described?

Institute for Food and Development Policy, "Nicaragua: Give Change a Chance," *Food First Action Alert*, 1984, pp. 1,2.

The Sandinistas' emphasis on primary health care—mass immunizations, improved sanitation, free health care centers in poor areas—prompted the World Health Organization to designate Nicaragua a model country.

We understand the desire of many Americans to avoid endorsing a political process that may not meet all their standards. We hope to show that the responsibility of Americans wanting to ally themselves with the cause of the hungry majority in Central America does not require any compromise of such a principled stance.

Five Difficult Lessons

Based on many years travel and research in the Third World, we at Food First have learned the following lessons regarding hunger and its relation to social conflict. First, in places like Central America, no amount of foreign aid or new technology can end hunger. The benefits of such assistance are monopolized by the elites who control the economy and government. Nothing less is required than a fundamental shift in power from a privileged elite to leadership accountable to the majority. Such a genuine shift in power is called "revolution." This is distinguished from a "coup", simply installing a new elite. Second, there will always be struggles for such revolutionary shifts in power. The hungry will not continue to watch their children die needlessly. Third, only the poor and their allies can create genuine revolutionary change: outsiders cannot do it for them. Fourth, the poor invariably begin their struggles through peaceful means, but when the privileged classes protect their status with force, revolutionary violence results. Fifth, there will always be counter-revolution. Once deposed from power, local elites and their foreign allies will mount attacks on the revolution, attempting to regain lost privileges.

It is not inevitable that the U.S. government support counter-revolutionary efforts. In the past this has been the case. But in the future, if we educate and mobilize the American people, we can prevent our government from in-

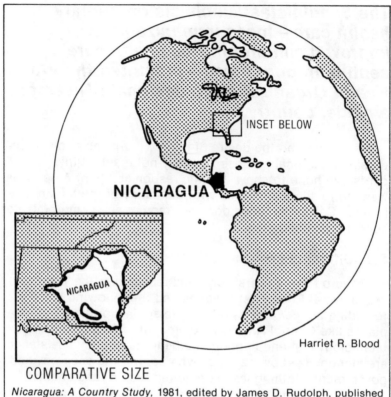

NICARAGUA

INSET BELOW

NICARAGUA

COMPARATIVE SIZE

Harriet R. Blood

Nicaragua: A Country Study, 1981, edited by James D. Rudolph, published by U.S. Government Printing Office for Department of the Army.

tervening on the side of the rich against the poor.

In this alert we will present some of the facts we have un-covered—most by first-hand observation—about revolu-tionary change in Nicaragua. We seek to show that the Nicaraguan revolution has both strengths and weaknesses, but the weaknesses should never justify U.S. efforts to over-throw that country's government.

Giving Priority to the Poor

Under the Somoza dictatorship, over half of Nicaragua's children were undernourished. Even in the best economic year (1977) over 90 percent of the deaths of children under one year were related to malnutrition.

The new government's programs have cut infant mortality by over one-third. The Sandinistas' emphasis on primary health care—mass immunizations, improved sanitation, free health care centers in poor areas—prompted the World Health Organization to designate Nicaragua a model country. "Before, almost every day a little coffin would come by in a funeral procession," reports Sister Pat Edmiston, a Maryknoll nurse working in a poor barrio. "Now you don't see that."

Under the Somoza dictatorship, over half of all Nicaraguans could neither read nor write. In many rural areas 100 percent of the women were illiterate. But in 1980, a universally praised literacy campaign cut the illiteracy rate to 13 percent. Over 1400 new schools have been built, mainly in rural areas. School enrollment has more than doubled, and 200,000 adults now participate in evening classes. Everywhere in the countryside one encounters previously illiterate peasants proudly keeping farm ledgers.

The theme of Nicaragua's agrarian reform is "idle land to working hands." By July 1984, titles to over one-fifth of the nation's farmland had been granted, free of charge, to over 45,000 land-poor families. Total land now owned by peasants, including the 2.4 million acres given away under the agrarian reform, amounts to *ten times* that held by peasants under the Somoza dynasty.

The goal of the reform—now within sight—is to provide land for everyone who wants a farm. In a major social advance, women are receiving titles to their own land.

Also in contrast to land reforms in other countries, Nicaragua's places no ceiling on the amount of land anyone can own. It requires only that farmland be used; land not being used efficiently is subject to redistribution to the landless.

Government policy has not favored the state farms, formed from the large estates Somoza abandoned in 1979. Many state farms have been titled over to cooperatives and individual peasant families.

But land is useless without credit to buy seeds, tools and fertilizer. So the government is also providing peasant producers with ample credit and technical assistance.

As one peasant woman told us: "It's very different now. Before, a lot of people went hungry. People were so in debt they had to mortgage their crops. Now people get credit from the government. Now people can eat three times a day."

Ending the Suffering

If they survive the first year of life, Central American children face malnutrition and unsanitary conditions. About three-fourths of all Salvadoran children under the age of five are malnourished...According to the most recent statistics available on Guatemala, 94 percent of the people there receive no schooling at all..Nicaragua still has poverty but the situation there is distinct from what is found in the rest of Central America, and some explanation is necessary.

The Sandinista government early established ending the suffering of the poor as its highest priority. Any such policy must attack poor health, education and housing. Thousands of U.S. church people have visited Nicaragua and given witness to remarkable achievements...

Official figures show that, in the past six years, infant mortality has dropped from 122 to between 50 and 80 deaths for every 1,000 births—still high but moving in the right direction. (The U.S. rate is 11 per 1,000.) Life expectancy under the Sandinistas, according to the government's health ministry, has risen from 53 years to 58, and is projected to reach 65 by the year 2000. And in 1983, the World Health Organization called Nicaragua a "model country in health care."

Nicaragua's successful literacy campaign has been widely reported. Not only are the children learning to read at last, but children have been organized to teach adults...

Sandinista reforms are succeeding despite immense economic and military pressure from Washington. If Nicaragua is indeed a threat to U.S. interests (as President Reagan asserts), it is a threat because of the hope its example gives to the poor. Hope is a gift that the poor seldom receive, and it threatens the dominant economic interests (local and foreign) of Central America.

Rob Cogswell, *The Christian Century,* May 8, 1985.

U.S. War is Creating an Emergency

These significant advances in health, education and land reform are jeopardized by the U.S.-directed war being waged by counterrevolutionaries ("contras") based in Honduras and Costa Rica. Because of contra attacks, 25 percent of the national budget must be diverted to defense. As of July 1984, no new projects in health or education could be undertaken.

There has been a sharp decline in corn and bean production, located primarily in areas under contra attack. The Sandinistas are determined to prevent war-related shortages from enriching those who hoard goods and speculate on people's basic needs. In August 1984, the government began rationing eight essential products to ensure fair distribution. Rationing, welcomed by many poor Nicaraguans victimized by speculators, is resented by many merchants who believe it restricts their profits.

Thus rationing will entail stiffer laws and stricter police enforcement which the Reagan administration will no doubt seize upon as another way of discrediting the Sandinistas.

A Policy of Aggression

Despite numerous polls showing the majority of U.S. citizens oppose the policy, Congress and the Administration have given more than $70 million to the contras based in Honduras and Costa Rica.

For the past three years contra forces, led by former members of Somoza's hated National Guard, have carried out terrorist raids, targeting whoever symbolizes the new Nicaragua: a rural nurse, an adult education teacher, a student volunteering to pick coffee, a peasant family which received land through the agrarian reform.

Financed and directed by the CIA and Pentagon, the contras have killed and wounded over 7,000 people, many of them unarmed civilians and even children. Contra attacks have caused an estimated $250 million in property damage, over one-half the country's annual export earnings. By burning peasant farms, granaries, tractors and trucks, the contras have undermined Nicaragua's food supply.

Because of massive U.S. military assistance, the contras are able to step up their attacks despite their conspicuous lack of popular support or military success.

3 PROPONENTS' FORUM

ECONOMIC ACHIEVEMENTS
OF THE
REVOLUTION

Republic of Nicaragua

The following statistics and data were provided by the Nicaraguan Embassy in Washington D.C. The data on the achievements of the revolution is taken from Nicaraguan Fact Sheets published by the National Government of Reconstruction and presents the perspective of the San-dinista National Liberation Front - FSLN (Frente Sandinista de Liberacion Nacional). The first part of this reading presents an overview of the Sandinista reforms by the Com-mittee of Returned Peace Corps Volunteers.

Points to Consider

1. How do the returned peace corps volunteers describe conditions under Somoza?
2. What do they say about the Sandinistas?
3. Describe the most important features of the education, agrarian, health, housing and welfare reforms.
4. What percent of land was privately owned after the revolution?

"Nicaraguan Fact Sheet," published by the Republic of Nicaragua.

Although under constant attack and threat of attack, the Sandinistas have made impressive strides.

Nicaragua is the largest country in Central America and the only one to mount a successful popular revolution, in 1979. Commonly referred to as the "Sandinistas," Nicaragua's new government has chosen to follow a policy of non-alignment, a striking contrast to the full cooperation the United States received from the previous dictatorship of the Somoza family (1933-1979).

Within Nicaragua, the Somoza family controlled most of the wealth of Nicaragua and a land area the size of Massachusetts. The literacy rate was under 50 percent, and half of all rural infants died before reaching the age of four. Somoza used the U.S.-formed-and-trained National Guard as his personal army following the departure of the U.S. marines who had occupied Nicaragua from 1911 to 1933 and placed his family in power. All of our respondents agree that the years of underdevelopment, the terror and looting of the Somoza regime, and foreign domination sowed the seeds of an inevitable revolution.

The Sandinistas allied with the middle class, business groups, and the Catholic Church to overthrow Anastasio Somoza and form a coalition government. The Carter Administration recognized the new government and initially authorized an economic aid package. However, in 1981, the Reagan Administration, worried by the presence of Marxists in the coalition, reversed the policy and began covert destabilization operations. Since 1981, the United States has spent millions of dollars to arm and train Somoza loyalists and disenchanted Sandinistas for invasion.

Although under constant attack and threat of attack, the Sandinistas have made impressive strides. In the first 18 months, they reduced inflation from 84 percent to 27 percent and unemployment from 40 percent to 16 percent. Illiteracy has fallen from 52 percent to 13 percent, and infant mortality has been greatly reduced. A vaccination campaign has recently eradicated polio and drastically reduced malaria. The World Health Organization chose Nicaragua as one of five model countries in terms of its primary health care delivery system.

The Sandinistas appealed to the international community for economic assistance. The U.S. government answered by encouraging an economic boycott and by launching a "secret war" from Honduras. Twenty of our 21 respondents feel that the United States should support the Sandinistas and that the present U.S. military threat serves only to push them further to the left.[1]

Progress In Nicaragua

(The following data compares the economic and social advances made by the Sandinistas with the economic and social conditions in 1978 under Somoza before the revolution. This data is provided by the Nicaraguan Government.)

EDUCATION THEN	EDUCATION NOW
Education was available only to those who had the means to pay.	Education is completely free.
1978: 50.3% illiteracy	1980: 12.9% illiteracy
1978: 24,000 students in higher education.	35,000 students in higher education.
1978: 501,660 students in middle school.	1,127,428 students in middle school.
1978: 9,000 children in pre-school.	66,850 children in pre-school.
1978: 369,640 students in elementary school.	635,637 students in elementary school.
No data available.	A national total of 53,398 teachers at all levels of education.
1978: 5 Teacher-Training Schools.	14 Teacher-Training Schools.

1. Excerpted from "Voice of Experience in Central America," written by former Peace Corps Volunteers, January 5, 1985.

1978: 1 special education school.	25 special education schools.
1978: 1,500 scholarships for study abroad.	5,576 scholarships for study abroad.
Non-existent.	17,000 Adult Education Collectives.
Non-existent	22,000 community teachers
No data available.	2,000 elementary schools.
No data available.	14 technical education centers.
No data available.	800 community schools..
1978: 2 universities.	4 universities
No data available.	24 rural education units.
No data available.	130 graduate-level and technical university fields of specialization.
1978: National education budget of 341 million cordobas.	2 billion cordobas assigned to education from the National Budget.

HEALTH CARE THEN

HEALTH CARE NOW

1978: Private health care available only to well-to-do sectors of the population.	National Health Care Service created.
1978: Nicaragua never received any international recognition.	1983: The World Health Organization named Nicaragua ''the model Country in Health Care.''
1977: Infant mortality was 121 deaths for every 1000 children.	1983: The infant mortality rate was reduced to 75 deaths for every 1000 live births.

1977: No oral rehydration programs available; this was one of the causes of infant mortality.	290 Oral Rehydration Units provided for children.
1977: 1,006,563 vaccinations given.	1983: 3,495,431 vaccinations given.
1977: 2.4 million medical consultants	6.4 million medical consultants.
1977: One nursing school.	5 nursing schools.
1977: Five teaching hospitals.	21 teaching hospitals.
1978: Life expectancy of 55 years.	1983: Life expectancy of 58 years.
1977: 3% of the national budget allocated to health care.	1983: 11% of the national budget allocated to health care.
1978: No data available.	5 new hospitals built.
1978: No data available.	309 Health Centers created.
1978: The public does not participate in vaccination campaigns.	160,000 brigadeers participate in the vaccination campaigns.

Polio Gone from Nicaragua

For the first time in the history of Nicaragua, the scourge of poliomyelitis has disappeared completely. Nicaragua's Ministry of Health is determined to repeat this 1982-1983 victory again in 1984 and even after. A total of 500,000 children, from newborns to six years of age, 200,000 of them in Managua alone, were scheduled to receive the oral polio vaccine drops on Sunday, February 12, 1984.

Regina Pustan, *U.S. Farm News*, February, 1985.

1978: There were no Environmental Hygiene Campaigns.	Various Environmental Hygiene Campaigns are carried out.
1978: 150 medical students.	550 medical students.

1977: The following quantity of students are registered for medical training:

Advanced Technicians............0
Health Aides....................0
Nurses.........................60
Doctors.......................135
Clinical-Surgical Specialists........0

The following number of students are registered for medical training:

Advanced Technicians..........336
Health Aides................1161
Nurses......................600
Doctors.....................550
Clinical-Surgical Specialists......135

AGRARIAN REFORM THEN

AGRARIAN REFORM NOW

1978: More than 50% of land held in latifundia.

The latifundia are reduced to 13% of landholdings.

1978: 120,000 owned 3% of the land.

The peasants own 44% of the land.

1977: 178,629 cordobas extended in rural credit.

1,600,395,000 cordobas have been extended in credit in the country's rural zones.

1978: Peasants lost their land due to progressive indebtedness.

328 million cordobas allocated to indemnify the peasant landowners' debts.

1979: 22 agricultural and livestock cooperatives with 1,240 members.

3,000 agricultural and livestock cooperatives with 70,000 members.

1979: 175 non-agricultural cooperatives with 5,854 members.

423 non-agricultural cooperatives benefitting 50,953 members.

Land ownership breaks down in the following way:

State-owned.................23%
Cooperative sector............7%
Private sector...............11%
Medium-scale landowners......30%
Small-scale landowners.........7%

SOCIAL SECURITY AND WELFARE THEN	SOCIAL SECURITY AND WELFARE NOW
1977: 4 day care centers	25 Child Development Centers, servicing 3,186 children.
1978: No childcare facilities in the country.	24 Rural Children's Service Centers which deliver care to 2,169 children.
1978: No Children's Cafeterias in the rural areas.	32 Children's Cafeterias which provide meals for 5,696 children in the rural areas.
1978: One Old-Age Home.	4 Old-Age Homes.
1978: The elderly were left destitute.	There are Work and Cultural Centers for the Retired.
1978: No programs for refugees.	National Refugee Program.
1979: No data available.	4 Social Rehabilitation Centers, attending 286 people.
1978: Social Security coverage available only in Managua.	1980: Extension of the Social Security coverage to the urban and rural populations: 929,909 insured.
1979: No data available.	Aid program benefitting 146,308 people.
1978: No optical services available at public health facilities.	1983: Creation of the Juan Carlos Herrera Health Service Opticians.
1978: No vacation programs.	1983: Vacation programs at resort centers.
1978: No Social Security coverage in the countryside.	1980: Social Security system extended to the countryside, benefitting 28,000 peasants.

PROPONENTS' FORUM

AGRICULTURE: PILLAR OF THE REVOLUTION

Michael Baumann

Michael Baumann is a correspondent for Intercontinental Press, *which has a full-time press bureau in Managua.* Intercontinental Press *features events of interest to socialist and liberation movements.*

Points to Consider

1. What and how much does Nicaragua's agriculture produce?
2. What was agriculture like before the revolution?
3. Describe the agricultural transformation that took place after the revolution.
4. What role does capitalism play in agriculture?

Michael Baumann, "Agriculture: A Pillar of the Revolution," *Intercontinental Press,* March 19, 1984, pp. 135-37.

"If the revolution has benefited any social sector in this society it has been the peasantry, and they have benefited greatly."

Agriculture is, and will remain for the forseeable future, the motor force of the Nicaraguan economy. It is the country's main source of hard currency, accounting for 70 percent of all exports ($350 million out of $500 million in 1981). Yet it absorbs only 10 percent of all imports. (Nicaragua's industry, for comparison, produces only $80 million in export income but requires twice that amount each year in imported raw and semi-finished materials.)

Nicaragua's agriculture produces most of the food consumed in the country, provides the bulk of public revenue, and absorbs the majority of public investment. The main urban centers are dependent on this agricultural base, which provides either raw materials or a market for three-quarters of the country's industry. More than two-thirds of the country's economically active population (630,000 out of 900,000) is estimated to be employed in agriculture. . .

"If the revolution has benefited any social sector in this society it has been the peasantry, and they have benefited greatly," agrarian reform minister Jaime Wheelock commented in a recent interview. "That is why the great majority of those who defend the revolution, with arms in hand, against the Somozaists are peasants."

To grasp the degree of backwardness U.S.-supported regimes imposed on rural Nicaragua for decades, it is useful to begin with one eloquent fact: in much of Nicaragua even the plow is unknown. According to an estimate by Wheelock, a majority of the country's basic food crops "are produced by peasants using technology at the same level as that of the Indians at the arrival of Columbus—the digging stick". . . .

Roots of Backwardness

The culprit was coffee, and later cotton. Not the crops themselves, but the way the peasantry was uprooted and dispersed to make room for them.

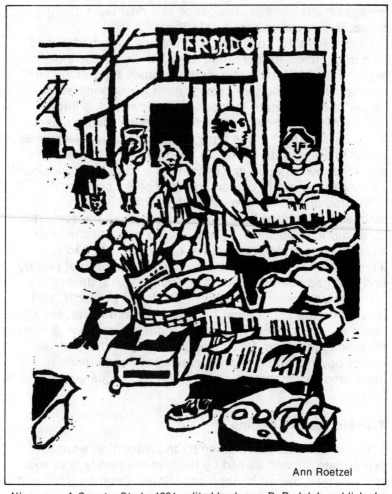

Ann Roetzel

Nicaragua: A Country Study, 1981, edited by James D. Rudolph, published by U.S. Government Printing Office for Department of the Army.

Cultivation of coffee was introduced in the 1870's. It became the dominant export crop after World War I and remains such today, accounting for about 40 percent of all export income. Large-scale cotton cultivation was introduced in the early 1950's.

Like all such abrupt changes under capitalism, introduction of these new crops brought wrenching social consequences. In the case of coffee, favorable prices on the world market resulted in the emergence of a new layer of entrepreneurs with an unquenchable thirst for land.

Tenant farmers, squatters, and Indians, who had owned land in common for centuries, were the first to be violently expropriated. Hit hard next were the small food producers, traditionally located just outside each major population center to compensate for poor transportation facilities.

Tens of thousands of small farmers were dispossessed. Many became part of the army of agricultural workers needed for three months a year during the harvest. Others retreated toward marginal, unclaimed land in the agricultural frontier to the north, center, and east of the country.

Nicaragua's coffee growers, Wheelock concludes, cold-bloodedly "destroyed the basis of agriculture for domestic consumption" because "it took up too much of the labor force in the countryside." In the process, "they had to almost totally dismember the system of agricultural production that had been handed down from colonial times."

It is the descendants of these displaced peasants, still located on the agricultural frontier—far from roads, storage facilities, or technical help—who today are producing most of Nicaragua's food. Rectifying the consequences of this forced population shift is ultimately the key to many of the most pressing problems faced in the Nicaraguan countryside today.

Transformation Begins

Two of the first steps taken by the revolution were to expropriate all land owned by the Somoza family, and soon after, all land owned by their associates (Decrees No. 3 and 38).

These two measures alone gave the state control over 2.8 million acres of some of the most modern agricultural units in the country. Almost all, however, were in the form of agro-export plantations and were not divided up among the landless peasants. To meet the peasants' needs for more land a later decree, confiscating all idle land, was necessary.

Immediate tasks on the big expropriated units were to revive production, which had been shattered by the war and by last-minute looting by departing owners. Many workers had not been paid in months, and most records had disappeared along with the former owners.

To restore production, tens of millions of dollars were pumped into the countryside by the newly nationalized banking system. Cheap and abundant credit was granted not only to the new state farms, but also to efficient big growers and peasants. The latter were encouraged to form cooperatives, both because of the long-range advantages of collective labor and to reduce the problem of providing aid to tens of thousands of individual producers.

Within two years, enormous progress was already visible. With the exception of cotton, production of cash crops reached acceptable levels of recovery by 1981. In the case of coffee, the 1982-83 harvest was the largest in the country's history. Banana production is now above the Somoza-era levels, and sugar and beef exports are equal to the best years under the dictatorship. . .

To continue and expand these gains, the revolutionary government has turned on its head the economic policy of

The Greatest Achievement

Agrarian Reform is perceived by Nicaraguans as the single greatest achievement of the revolution, prior to which the campesinos were forgotten. Today, they are taking their rightful place in society and the life of the country. Seventy percent of the Nicaraguan population are campesinos, and 75% of the country's foreign exchange comes from agroexports. Although the transformation process is slow and the Land Reform Law is Latin America's most conservative, significant accomplishments have been made. Since 1979, 15,000 peasant families have received land titles—850 coastal acres and 1,700 interior acres. Campesinos now own 19% of the cultivated land, the State owns 20%, and the private owners 61%. This redistribution of agricultural resources undoubtedly has contributed to Nicaragua's growth.

Jennie Baer & Marcia McLane, *Women's International League For Peace And Freedom,* December, 1983.

the Somoza dictatorship. Instead of focusing on the cities, it is concentrating some 80 percent of all productive investment in the countryside.

Economic reality, Wheelock explained to a recent international conference in Managua, has forced Nicaragua to take a hard look at investment priorities. "We must seek an alternative model of development," he said, "agro-industrialization—the processing of our own raw materials."

Instead of simply continuing to export raw or semi-finished food and fiber, "we have to begin to exploit our own resources, in a reasonable way, primarily through the processing of our agricultural production. This is the vital center of the economic and development strategy that has been drawn up by the National Directorate of the Sandinista National Liberation Front and by the Government of National Reconstruction."

Given the shortage of resources, Wheelock acknowledged, this can only be done at the expense of other priorities, including expansion of social services.

"Of course we are aware that our children are still barefoot," he said. "We know there is great poverty in the marginal barrios, that more health care and housing is needed. But we could fill the entire country with houses and provide shoes for every child—and this would still not resolve the problem of backwardness and underdevelopment. . . . We have to go to the root of the problem, not its peripheral aspects."

Most, but not all, of such increased investment will be on state-owned farms and processing facilities. Also envisioned are joint projects with capitalist agricultural producers.

Small in number but important economically, the big-business agricultural sector today accounts for half the country's production of sugar, rice, and cotton, and about a third of the coffee. They are sometimes jokingly referred to as "capitalists of a new type"—capitalists who have continued to function in a society where the workers and farmers wield political power.

Nicaragua's agarian reform places no limit on the amount of land a private producer may own—so long as it is fully used. Consequently there still remains a significant sector of large landowners—probably a few thousand—who were never directly connected with Somoza and thus were not confiscated.

THE CRITICS' FORUM

IMPLEMENTING SOCIALISM

U.S. Department of State

The following comments were excerpted from a State Department publication dealing with misconceptions about U.S. policy toward Nicaragua.

Points to Consider

1. How is the FSLN leadership described?
2. What is their relationship to communist countries?
3. How is the economic crisis defined?
4. What social programs were enacted by the Sandinistas?
5. How successful were these programs?

United States Department of State, "Misconceptions About U.S. Policy Toward Nicaragua," June, 1985.

Sandinista policies which emphasize Marxist ideology over economic realities are the root cause of Nicaragua's economic deterioration.

In 1979, the Nicaraguan people overthrew the Somoza dictatorship. The Sandinista National Liberation Front (FSLN), which led the military struggle, pledged that it would promote political pluralism, a mixed economy, and a nonaligned foreign policy. Since 1979, the Sandinistas have steered the revolution toward Marxism-Leninism, leaving their original promises unfulfilled. The U.S. Government sought from the outset to build a positive relationship with the new Government of National Reconstruction (GRN), but as the Sandinistas made clear that they had no intention of fulfilling their earlier promises, relations between the two nations deteriorated.

FSLN Leadership

The FSLN leadership is composed of committed revolutionaries who openly embrace Marxist-Leninist ideology. They claim to be a vanguard party with a historic right to lead the Nicaraguan people to "socialism" (read: communism). The Sandinistas condemn the United States as the center of capitalism and imperialism and thus the principal obstacle to world revolution. The FSLN hymn proclaims the Sandinista commitment to fight against "the Yankee, enemy of humanity."

In a secret speech made in the spring of 1984 to the Nicaraguan Socialist Party (PSN), a Moscow-line Communist party, Sandinista National Directorate member and political coordinator Bayardo Arce acknowledged that the FSLN had never intended to comply with its promises to promote pluralism, a mixed economy, and non-alignment. Arce explained that the FSLN had made these commitments simply to gain international support and thereby forestall possible U.S. intervention. He referred to the elections as "a nuisance" and described the FSLN's goal of building a Socialist Nicaragua with "a dictatorship of the proletariat."

Arce closed his speech appealing for "the unity of the Marxist-Leninists of Nicaragua."

The Sandinistas' fraternal relations with the Communist government of Cuba are based both on ideology and the long history of Cuban support for the FSLN. The Sandinistas regard Fidel Castro as their mentor. Not only did he furnish them with a model for their revolution, Castro also provided shelter and training during their 18 years of struggle against Somoza, and he supplied them with the weapons for their final offensive in 1979. Castro has continually coached the Sandinistas, and he even brokered the arrangement among the three FSLN factions which led to the formation of the current National Directorate in March 1979.

Economic Crisis

Sandinista policies which emphasize Marxist ideology over economic realities are the root cause of Nicaragua's economic deterioration. While the Sandinistas have paid lip service to a mixed economy, they have placed an ever greater portion of the economy under direct government control. Even the half of the economy still in private hands is subject to strict government regulation.

Sandinista anti-private sector policies such as confiscations—often used to punish political opponents—high taxes, declining internal financial credit, and stringent controls on prices, wages, and foreign exchange have strangled private enterprise, discouraged production, and prompted many Nicaraguan business leaders, managers, and professionals to go into exile.

These misguided policies have exacerbated the problems caused by war damage during the revolution and the world economic recession. Today, the per capita Gross National Product is 25% below the 1977 pre-revolutionary level and exports have declined 70% in real terms. The foreign debt has tripled from $1.6 to $4.6 billion in less than 6 years, and Nicaragua is seriously in arrears in debt repayments to most of its major creditors. The Nicaraguan people are suffering from growing shortages of food and basic consumer goods, an inflation rate of more than 60%, a one-third drop in real wages in the past 3 years, and more than 20% unemployment.

Source: U.S. Department of State

38

The United States initially supported assistance to Nicaragua in international financial institutions, and for 18 months provided more bilateral economic aid than any other country to Nicaragua. Not until May 1985 did the United States impose trade sanctions on Nicaragua in response to the Sandinistas' unceasing efforts to subvert their neighbors, their destabilizing military buildup, their close ties to the Soviet bloc, and their imposition of non-democratic rule.

Limited Economic Opportunity

Older Nicaraguans, particularly educated professionals, said their departures demonstrate a spreading assessment that private-sector economic opportunities are becoming limited. One businessman who resisted leaving mostly out of patriotism said he has decided to emigrate because "we have reached the point of no return" in the 5-year-old Sandinista revolution.

Many businessmen and professionals, particularly those from wealthy families associated with former dictator Anastasio Somoza, left soon after the Sandinista takeover in July 1979. But those leaving now appear to include younger professionals who had embraced the ideals of the revolution but have begun to despair of obtaining professional fulfillment or providing well for their families.

Edward Cody, *Washington Post,* April, 1985

The Social Programs

The Sandinista seizure of power in 1979 aroused hopes that the Nicaraguan people would soon enjoy a democratic government which would promote social justice and improve the quality of their lives. The Sandinistas, utilizing vast amounts of foreign aid—much of it from the United States—announced a number of programs, including a literacy campaign, construction of clinics, and expanded medical care. The programs were announced with much fanfare, and the Sandinista press releases describing the "miraculous" successes of these programs were generally repeated uncritically by the international press.

Had the Sandinistas fulfilled their promises to the Nicaraguan people for better lives and had the new government evolved toward a social democratic system, they possibly might have developed a model that could be emulated. Today none of Nicaragua's neighbors desire to voluntarily copy the Sandinista system. Instead, they fear attempts by force of arms to impose that system on their countries.

The widely touted literacy and health programs launched by the Sandinistas have not worked as people hoped. To sustain progress in combating adult illiteracy, a continuing effort is required. Initial gains are disappearing for lack of followup and the unavailability of interesting and uncensored reading material. The people are tired of the Marxist propaganda material made available to them in the guise of instructional material. The quality of instruction in the educational system has decreased. In 1983 only a small percentage of graduating secondary school students could pass a standardized examination. This lowering of academic standards is attributable in part to the injection of massive doses of Sandinista political propaganda into the educational program and to the conscription of school age children into the military.

While some advances have been made in preventive health care, the quality of curative medicine in Nicaragua has fallen sharply. The Sandinistas' repressive policies have driven many Nicaraguan doctors, nurses, and medical technicians into exile. Nicaraguans complain that the Cuban personnel who provide much of the medical service in Nicaragua today are poorly trained.

Similarly, the Sandinista claims of expansion of the number of trade unions have not improved the lot of the workers. The creation of new unions under Sandinista control has been a ruse to repress and destroy the free trade unions. The International Labor Organization in March 1984 expressed "serious concern" over the large number of trade unionists and employee representatives arrested and noted that "freedom of association can only be exercised" where fundamental human rights and "freedom from arbitrary arrest are fully respected and guaranteed." Many former trade union leaders have gone into exile.

Despite billions of dollars of foreign aid since 1979, per capita income in Nicaragua has declined to the levels of the early 1960s. Inflation is soaring—an estimated 100% in 1984 alone—and workers' wages continually decline in purchasing power.

Whereas Nicaragua, prior to 1979, was a net exporter of foodstuffs, it is now a net importer of food. Production has dropped and Nicaraguans are facing serious shortages of food as well as basic consumer goods. Food is rationed. The issuance of ration coupons by the local Sandinista Defense Committees (CDSs) has become a method of political pressure. Queues, typical of Eastern Europe, are now an everyday sight in Nicaraguan markets. Basic necessities often are available only on the black market at highly inflated prices. Peasant food producers often prefer selling to black market vendors who pay their bills.

In contrast to the poverty affecting Nicaraguan workers and peasants, the Sandinista elite drive luxury cars, and have followed the Soviet example of opening special stores where they can buy goods unavailable to the rest of the population. People elsewhere in Central America are not yearning to have the Nicaraguan model imposed upon them.

THE CRITICS' FORUM

TIME IS RUNNING OUT

John McLaughlin

John McLaughlin is an executive editor for the National
Review *and a prominent national spokesman for conservative causes and ideas.*

Points to Consider

1. What kind of economic erosion is described?
2. What economic institutions does the Sandinista Government control?
3. How is the "informer system" defined?
4. Why is time running out on the Sandinistas?

The principal seeds of the dissolution, however, lie in the economy, which, more than anything else, is causing this government to erode.

Managua. What greets you when you first arrive at the Managua airport is a sign saying that foreigners are required to exchange $60 into Nicaraguan cordobas to enter the country. This is a tipoff to the country's most alarming vulnerability, economic erosion. The Sandinistas badly need hard currency. The official rate of exchange is ten cordobas to the dollar, but you can get one hundred to the dollar on the black market, and 28 on the legal "parallel" market.

Food is scarce. At the central shopping area, saleswomen stand next to half or wholly empty shelves. Food rationing has been mandated. A family typically gets six eggs a week. A full-sized tube of toothpaste sells for $25. Inflation is now hitting 35 per cent and unemployment 17 per cent. An unskilled worker earns about 1,500 cordobas a month; a pair of shoes would cost him one-third of that.

Nicaragua's foreign debt stands at $3.2 billion at present, with its interest unpaid, and foreign reserves at minus $450 million. Before the Sandinista revolution (1978), the share of the GNP dedicated to the public sector was 15 percent; today it is about 50 per cent. This has meant catastrophic losses in industrial production; agricultural production is back up somewhat, however, but not to the levels of 1970 through 1975. Although the Russians are pumping funds into the economy, this injection is for a few big projects, with little ameliorative effect on the everyday economy. Arturo Cruz, once the director of Nicaragua's Central Bank and a member of the Sandinista junta (he is the one defector whom the Comandantes still treat with kid gloves, hoping to woo him back), has concluded that "Nicaragua is condemned to be an international beggar."

From July 1979 to August 1983, the U.S. delivered $135 million in economic aid to Nicaragua. The Sandinistas' own figures indicate that they received $500 million in multilateral and bilateral assistance each year from 1980 through 1982 (the last year for which figures are available), totaling $1.5 billion. Despite this mammoth transfusion, the Sandinista-run economy is staggering, and, if Ronald Reagan has his way, it will be given the coup de grace. We have ended our own aid and routinely try to block multinational loans, like the Inter-American Development Bank's recent $30 million to revive Nicaragua's fisheries, which, despite our veto, somehow made it through.

Economic Mismanagement

Today in Nicaragua, the banner of Sandinismo is giving way to the reality of communism. Since 1979, the Sandinistas have consolidated control over the government and the armed forces. They have placed under direct state control nearly half of Nicaragua's industry and 40% of its agriculture. By the selective application of monetary and labor laws, they exert pressure against the remainder of the industrial and agricultural sectors. The Sandinistas control all media outlets through censorship. . .

Neighborhood watch committees, informant networks, rationing of many basic necessities, and enforced participation in Sandinista organizations are all used to control and intimidate the people.

The Sandinistas' economic mismanagement, human rights violations, and abuse of governmental authority have driven more than 120,000 Nicaraguans into exile (some estimates range far higher). An even greater reflection of popular discontent has been the number of Nicaraguan citizens who have taken up arms against the Sandinistas.

U.S. State Department, *The Soviet-Cuban Connection In Central America,* March, 1985

Can this bird fly?

A War of Nerves

The Sandinistas tell you that they have a mixed economy, but you discover shortly from talking to tradesmen that neither wages nor prices can be changed without government clearance, even at small mom-and-pop businesses way out in the country. The revolutionary government today owns the banks; it controls all the nation's basic products, from cosmetics to cement; it runs the export trade. This means that business investment and incentive have shriveled, and an ever-growing stream of entrepreneurs, skilled workers, and professionals is flowing out of the country.

The grousing that all of this provokes among the people is pervasive, as you can imagine, and requires systematic social control to be held in check. So the classic, telltale, Communist police-state regimen is all in place. First, communications are locked up. You look in vain for a foreign newspaper, even at the Inter-Continental Hotel. The official local papers, *Barricada* and *Nuevo Diario,* are both available, of course, but so pro-Sandinista as to be comic. *La Prensa,* edited by the audacious Pedro Chamorro, is critical of the government, but is carefully censored before publication. The one TV news program that is aired is a joke.

Politically, a few non-Sandinista parties exist, like the Democratic Conservatives, but they can neither assemble nor recruit, and are little more than symbolic. Nicaraguans who criticize the government are subject to arrest. The most sickening aspect of the Communization process is the informer system that is being erected under the direction of imported East Germans, with neighborhood bloc leaders and Sandinista Defense Committees (CDS). The CDS unit leaders, by the way, are the same friendly folk who give you your food ration cards and, when there is one, your job. If you want to eat, you'd better be pro-revolution.

The third impression that jumps out at you in this environment is the war of nerves. The nine-man junta that runs the country is preoccupied by and, intermittently, jittery about the three insurgencies on their borders. Anti-Sandinista counter-revolutionaries are active in three areas: eight thousand *contras* to the north (the *Frente Democratico Nicaraguense)* staging hit-and-run forays at the border, reaching as far south as the Matagalpa province, northeast of Managua; two thousand *contras* in the southwest (the *Alianza Revolucionaria Democratica)*, under Comandante Cero (the former Sandinista, Eden Pastora), controlling a strip of territory along the San Juan River, which separates Nicaragua from Costa Rica; and two thousand Miskito and other Indians in the northeast, headed by thirty-year-old Stedman Fagoth, whose American father married a Miskito Indian. The Sandinista regime is forced to counter these insurgencies, meaning that 25,000 army regulars and special forces have to be fully mobilized, fed, housed, and clothed. The newly instituted draft aimed at pressing 200,000 youths into the service by year's end will exact still more costs.

Time Is Running Out

Some pro-Sandinistas here argue that the *contras* are only stiffening the spine of the populace, uniting it behind the revolution. And, indeed, they have caused a goodly number of the younger half of the population to rally patriotically behind the regime. But there is no question that the *contras* have had a destabilizing impact on both the government and the masses.

The principal seeds of the dissolution, however, lie in the economy, which, more than anything else, is causing this government to erode. One comes away with the feeling that since the Sandinistas show no sign of reform, since President Reagan (and Congress, it appears) is bent on maintaining the pressure, and since no deal is yet on the table or seems to be in the offing, the Sandinistas' string has perhaps six months to a year to run out. The unraveling is their own doing. The Comandantes have betrayed their revolution. Will their revolution now betray them?

THE CRITICS' FORUM

CHRONIC
ECONOMIC PROBLEMS

American Embassy in Nicaragua

The following article was taken from an economic analysis and forecast of the Nicaraguan economy by the staff of the American Embassy in Managua.

Points to Consider

1. What is the future outlook for the Nicaraguan economy?
2. Why is agriculture central to the economy?
3. How is the land reform described?
4. What role does Nicaraguan industry play?

Excerpted from "Foreign Economic Trends," American Embassy in Nicaragua, 1984.

The steady drain of trained managers and professionals continues. Together with shortages of resources for investment, this costly emigration spells a very gloomy picture for the Nicaraguan economy in years to come.

The Nicaraguan economy at best will show minimal growth, and the outlook for the medium term is not favorable. Among the chronic economic problems for which there is no early solution in view: A structural current account deficit in the range of $100 million per year, growing government control of all aspects of economic activity, a population and workforce expanding at 3.3 percent annually, acute shortages of skilled managers and workers combined with a glut of unskilled job seekers, declining commercial activity within the Central American Common Market, a poor business climate caused by property confiscations and the Marxist orientation of the Sandinista government, and increasingly active anti-Sandinista guerrilla movements in the frontier regions...

Agriculture is the backbone of the Nicaraguan economy, directly accounting for a quarter of the GDP (Gross Domestic Product) and indirectly for much more, since nearly half of industrial production involves the transformation of agricultural products. Together, cotton, coffee, sugar, and meat generate two thirds of Nicaragua's exports. Weak international prices for these commodities, combined with lower production, accounted for much of the decline in exports last year. Only in meat, where the herds were beginning to recover from the decimation suffered during the revolution, did export volume rise.

Land Reform

The GRN (Government of National Reconstruction) adopted an Agrarian Reform Law in August 1981, and since then has been engaged in redistributing land to Campesinos, mostly those organized into cooperatives. The state directly controls about 20 percent of the agricultural land in Nicaragua, which it seized from the Somoza family after the

49

revolution. Nicaragua's land reform problem differs from that in neighboring countries, such as El Salvador, because in Nicaragua there is plenty of land to go around. The competition is therefore not over land as such, but over developed infrastructure. Initially, the pace of land redistribution was slow, because the GRN did not have the technical and financial resources to support faster redistribution. Recently, however, the pace of land reform has accelerated significantly, particularly in the frontier regions where the GRN is trying to bolster its popularity among the Campesinos in the face of the counter-revolutionary threat. Land distributed by the government does not entitle the Campesino to sell or rent out his plot, and is frequently tied to his membership in a particular cooperative. Land reform titles may be inherited. The Sandinista government has stated that its long-run goal is to have 50 percent of the agricultural land in the hands of the cooperative sector, 25 percent in the hands of the state, and 25 percent in the hands of the private sector.

Much of the land that has been distributed under agrarian reform has been confiscated or expropriated from private owners. Under the Agrarian Reform Law, only those farms which are both large and which can be shown to be under-exploited are subject to confiscation or expropriation. This legal provision has in fact been applied politically in many cases, and increasingly overtly political confiscations have occurred: Adequate compensation has seldom been available for the victims of expropriation. This feature of Nicaraguan land reform has done much to inhibit private sector investment in agriculture, and thereby has hindered the recovery of production to pre-revolutionary levels.

Industry and Construction

Nicaraguan industry historically accounts for about a quarter of the country's GDP. Light industry (food products, textiles, wood products and chemicals) constitutes the bulk of the industrial base, which was created in the 1960's and oriented toward the Central American Common Market. This orientation, combined with the heavy dependence on imported inputs, explains the weak performance of Nicaraguan industry since the revolution. The government does not regard the majority of industry as a good candidate for investment, and except for textiles and food products, can be expected to allow it to languish. About 40 percent of the industrial sector is nationalized, a percentage likely to grow as further confiscations, the lack of private investment, and the nonprofitability of industry in general cull out private sector firms over time.

Construction is dominated by central government activity and depends upon the availability of foreign financing. Major projects are normally carried out with technical assistance from abroad. At the present time, the most important construction projects in Nicaragua (all official) are the

Chaotic Economy

Even supporters of the government agree that economic planning by the Sandinista *comandantes* is chaotic at best. An East German economist visiting Nicaragua lamented: "They [the Sandinistas] are about to propose a law that will set up about 15 separate exchange rates for imports and exports. I can't think of any East European economy as messed up as this one."

"Small farmers used to bring produce to the market or roadside and sell directly to the consumer. Now they have to sell it to the government for prices that discourage even back-yard farming. The government has become a burdensome middle man, sucking money and vitality out of the economy."

The Sandinista government explains that expenses associated with the war are to blame for shortages and the general economic deterioration of Nicaragua. But economic policies that discourage production remain in place and, even with the war, many question why the government admits to spending 40% of its budget on its 100,000-man army, but according to Jaime Chamorro, co-director of the independent newspaper La Prensa, the figure is probably well above 50%.

David Asman, *The Wall Street Journal,* March 25, 1985

Malacatoya Sugar Refinery (with assistance from Cuba), the Asturias Hydroelectric Project (with assistance from the IDB), the Port Expansion Project at El Bluff (with assistance from Bulgaria and Holland), the Momotombo Geothermal Project (with assistance from Italy and France), and the construction of a new textile factory (with assistance from Czechoslovakia).

The Outlook

The GRN has recently revised downward its projections for economic growth. Originally it had hoped for 6.6 real GDP growth, and is now predicting 3.4 percent. The revision was accompanied by warnings against overly optimistic predictions by economic ministries, and by indications that a particularly difficult year lies ahead for Nicaragua. In fact, the country will be fortunate to achieve zero growth this year. The good coffee and cotton harvests will not be enough to offset signs of declining production in industry, mining, fishing, and perhaps even cattle. The insurgency by counter-revolutionaries in the frontier regions has caused an officially estimated $70 million in infrastructure and production damage since late 1981. This has been difficult for the GRN, but not disastrous. Worse has been the increasing distraction of manpower, resources, and, above all, the attention of government leaders toward this conflict. The continuing economic difficulties necessarily receive less attention than they otherwise would.

The only bright spot appears to be cotton, where the GRN claims planted acreage is 15 percent above planned levels. In coffee, the late pains and problems with blight will cause production to fall by an estimated 14 percent, according to the government. Cattle will be badly hit by the failure of this year's sorghum crop. Poor harvests in basic grains (corn and sorghum) loom ahead, which will force scarce dollars to be used for imports. A major squeeze in external accounts is possible if foreign assistance drops. Given the ideology of the GRN, significant moves to improve the investment climate and stimulate private production are not likely. The steady drain of trained managers and professionals continues. Together with shortages of resources for investment, this costly emigration spells a very gloomy picture for the Nicaraguan economy in years to come.

INTERPRETING EDITORIAL CARTOONS

This activity may be used as an individualized study guide for students in libraries and resource centers or as a discussion catalyst in small group and classroom discussions.

Although cartoons are usually humorous, the main intent of most political cartoonists is not to entertain. Cartoons express serious social comment about important issues. Using graphic and visual arts, the cartoonist expresses opinions and attitudes. By employing an entertaining and often light-hearted visual format, cartoonists may have as much or more impact on national and world issues as editorial and syndicated columnists.

Points to Consider

1. Examine the two cartoons in this activity.(see next page)

2. How would you describe the message of each cartoon? Try to describe each message in one to three sentences.

3. Do you agree with the message expressed in either cartoon? Why or why not?

4. Do either of the cartoons support the author's point of view in any of the readings in this publication? If the answer is yes, be specific about which reading or readings and why.

5. Are any of the readings in chapter two in basic agreement with either of the cartoons?

53

Embargonomics

Gorbarukov, from Trud, Moscow

CHAPTER 3

HUMAN RIGHTS IN NICARAGUA

CONTRA TERROR, TORTURE AND MURDER

International Human Rights Law Group

A major report documenting scores of incidents of attacks on civilians by the contras in Nicaragua was released at a news conference on Capitol Hill called by The Washington Office on Latin America (WOLA), The International Human Rights Law Group and the office of Congressman Sam Gejdenson (D - Conn.), a member of the House Foreign Affairs Committee.

WOLA, the Law Group and Congressman Gejdenson together called for an immediate Congressional investigation of the abuses cited in the report, and the overall pattern of contra behavior in Nicaragua.

The report is based on 145 affidavits, signed under oath, from multiple eye-witnesses to over 75 incidents of contra brutality directed against civilians. It is the most extensive documentation yet to emerge on the conduct of the contra war.

The documentation in the report was assembled on a volunteer basis by attorney Reed Brody, a former Assistant Attorney General of the State of New York. Mr. Brody worked collecting the evidence in Nicaragua.

Points to Consider

1. How was the report on contra atrocities compiled?
2. What is the purpose of the attacks on civilians?
3. Who were the Barredas and what happened to them?

International Human Rights Law Group, "Attacks by the Nicaraguan Contras on the Civilian Population of Nicaragua," March, 1985.

Incidents reveal a distinct pattern, indicating that contra activities often include premeditated acts of brutality including rape, beatings, mutilation and torture.

For the past three years, counterrevolutionary armed forces, commonly known as "contras," have carried on a guerrilla war in Nicaragua. Although unable to capture or hold any sizeable town or populated area, the "contras" have inflicted numerous casualties and caused substantial damage to the Nicaraguan economy. That much has been widely reported. Recently, however, accounts have surfaced with increasing regularity, and from a variety of sources, that the contras are directing their attacks against civilian targets—such as workers in the northern provinces attempting to harvest the coffee crop—and that these attacks have resulted in assassination, torture, rape, kidnapping and mutilation of civilians.

To probe the veracity of these reports, a fact-finding team, led by an American lawyer who volunteered his time, spent from September 1984 to January 1985 in Nicaragua. The team set out to locate victims and other eyewitnesses to contra attacks throughout northern and north-central Nicaragua—including Nicaraguan peasants and workers, as well as U.S. priests, nuns and lay pastoral workers—interview them, and obtain sworn affidavits recounting in their own words what they had seen or experienced. This report contains the results of this investigation . . .

The investigation was structured to be as objective and professional as possible. A rigorous standard was applied: the report would include only those incidents and events that could be substantiated by reliable evidence of a kind that would be legally sufficient in a court of law. Thus, all of the facts presented here are based on direct eyewitness testimony . . .

In most cases, the account of one witness was corroborated by the similar accounts of as many as fifteen others. Where the credibility of a witness was considered doubtful for any reason, the statement was excluded from the report . . .

The interviews were conducted during several trips to the areas of Nicaragua where the contra attacks have been the heaviest . . .

A Distinct Pattern

Those incidents that have been investigated, however, reveal a distinct pattern, indicating that contra activities often include:

- attacks on purely civilian targets resulting in the killing of unarmed men, women, children and the elderly;
- premeditated acts of brutality including rape, beatings, mutilation and torture;
- individual and mass kidnapping of civilians—particularly in the northern Atlantic Coast region—for the purpose of forced recruitment into the contra forces and the creation of a hostage refugee population in Honduras;
- assaults on economic and social targets such as farms, cooperatives, food storage facilities and health centers, including a particular effort to disrupt the coffee harvests through attacks on coffee cooperatives and on vehicles carrying volunteer coffee harvesters;
- intimidation of civilians who participate or cooperate in government or community programs such as distribution of subsidized food products, education and the local self-defense militias; and
- kidnapping, intimidation, and even murder of religious leaders who support the government, including priests and clergy-trained lay pastors.

Following are some excerpts from the affidavits themselves:

- Digna Barreda de Ubeda, a mother of two from Esteli, was kidnapped by the contras in May 1983:

"Five of them raped me at about five in the evening . . . they had gang-raped me every day. When my vagina couldn't take it anymore, they raped me through my rectum. I calculate that in 5 days they raped me 60 times."

She also watched contra forces beat her husband and gouge out the eyes of another civilian before killing him.

- Doroteo Tinoco Valdivia, testifying about an attack in April 1984 on his farming cooperative near Yali, Jinotega:

"They had already destroyed all that was the cooperative; a coffee drying machine, the two dormitories for the coffee

The enemy approaches

cutters, the electricity generators, 7 cows, the plant, the food warehouse.

"There was one boy about 15 years old, who was retarded and suffered from epilepsy. We had left him in a bomb shelter.

"When we returned . . . we saw . . . that they had cut his throat, then they cut open his stomach and left his intestines hanging out on the ground like a string.

"They did the same to Juan Corrales who had already died from a bullet in the fighting. They opened him up and took out his intestines and cut off his testicles . . ."

- Mirna Cunningham, a Black Miskito Indian doctor who is now the government's Minister for the northern Atlantic coast, describing how she and a nurse were treated after being kidnapped by the contras in December 1981:

"During those hours we were raped for the first time. While they were raping us, they were chanting slogans like 'Christ yesterday, Christ today, Christ tomorrow . . . ' And although we would cry or shout, they would hit us, and put a knife or a gun to our head. This went on for almost two hours."

- Maria Bustillo viuda de Blandon told of how her husband, a lay pastor, and her five children were taken from her home near El Jicaro one night in October 1982; when she found them the next day:

"They were left all cut up. Their ears were pulled off, their throats were cut, their noses and other parts were cut off . . ."

- Inocente Peralta, a lay pastor, went out looking for seven people taken in an attack on a Jinotega cooperative in April 1984. He describes the condition in which the bodies were found; for example:

"We found (Juan Perez) assassinated in the mountains. They had tied his hands behind his back. They hung him on a wire fence. They opened up his throat and took out his tongue. Another bayonet had gone in through his stomach and come out his back. Finally they cut off his testicles. It was horrible to see."

Carmen Gutierrez described the death of her four year old daughter Suyapa in a June, 1983 mortar attack on her border town of Teotecacinte:

"When we were all in the (bomb) shelter, my mother asked if any of the children were missing, so we called them by their names. Only Suyapa was missing. I went out . . . Then I remembered that I had seen her playing with a hen. I went there and saw her dead. Her face was blown away but I didn't realize it, I didn't even notice the mortaring. I picked her up and ran away like mad. Then I realized that part of her face was missing. I went back to look and found the piece of

On the Warpath

The Reagan administration is on the warpath in Nicaragua. U.S. troops may not yet be in the frontlines, but Washington is financing and directing a paramilitary campaign that is taking lives, ravaging communities, and deliberately inflicting suffering on innocent Nicaraguans.

Richard J. Barnet & Peter Kornbluh, *Sojourners*, May 8, 1984.

her face."

- Orlando Wayland, a Miskito teacher who was kidnapped by the contras in December 1983, testifying to tortures applied to him and eight others in Honduras:

"In the evening, they tied me up in the water from 7 p.m. until 1 a.m. The next day, at 7 a.m. they began to make me collect garbage in the creek in my underwear, with the cold. The creek was really icey. I was in the creek for four hours . . .

"Then they threw me on the ant hill. Tied up, they put me chest-down on the ant hill. The (red) ants bit my body. I squirmed to try to get them off my body, but there were too many.

"I was on the ant hill ten minutes each day . . .

"They would beat me from head to heels. They would give me an injection to calm me a little. Then they would beat me again."

- Abelina Inestroza, a mother from Susucayan, testifying about events of the previous day in December 1984:

"They grabbed us, me and my sister . . . and raped us in front of the whole family. They turned out the lights and 2 of them raped me and 2 others raped my sister. They told us not to scream because they would kill us. They threatened us with their bayonets. They pointed their guns at the others in the house."

- Maria Julia Ortiz was hiding under the bed when the contras broke into her house near El Jicaro in October 1984 and killed her husband:

"They grabbed my husband and they beat him and broke his neck with a rifle. They took him out of the room by one of the doors which was destroyed and they bashed in his head with a rifle and they took out his eye.

"Then they threw him on the floor and they tied his hands and they cut his throat with a bayonet. He screamed and fought . . . and said that he didn't do anything worng, but they wouldn't let him speak and put a green cloth in his mouth . . ."

The Barredas were well known citizens of Esteli. Deeply religious, they were Delegates of the Word (lay pastors) and members of the Pastoral Council of the Diocese of Esteli. In the late 1960's and early 1970's they had organized Christian Family Movement retreats, taught courses on Christianity and helped form youth groups and cooperatives. During the insurrection against Somoza, they had worked with the Sandinista Front and helped build Christian base communities in Esteli. The following account describes the murder and torture of the Barredas and their associates:

In that jail, the prisoners were stripped.

"They manacled us, tied us, blindfolded us and strapped us to trees. Three days after we arrived, dona Mary (Barreda) arrived, quite beaten and hemorrhaging. She collapsed upon arriving due to the extenuation, the fatique and the blows. They also stripped her of everything. They strapped her to a tree next to us. Thus we spent two days and two nights, strapped to the trees, standing, naked, barefoot, in the mud, and under the rain. They kept harassing us, and whenever a counterrevolutionary or a guardsman passed by he would threaten us with bayonets against our necks, against our chests, cursed us and slapped us in the face. They kept saying: 'Don't worry, for tonight you'll be dead. Don't worry, for tonight we are going to slit your throats. Right against those very trees, that's where you are going to die.'

The following night, still naked, they threw us into a gully, into a crevice. We moaned from the cold, the pain, the rain, the mud; the Barreda couple as well as the rest. Two days later they pulled us out of there. They interrogated them and us, they accused us, they beat us.

After five or six days of blows, torture, insults, interrogation, they said they would give us an opportunity to preserve our lives. They untied us, took our blinds off, and dressed us in U.S.-made suits: camouflage caps, camouflage brown and green jackets, jungle boots and pants. They placed machine-guns, FAL rifles, all sorts of weapons on our chests, across our chests we had to wear them. We were photographed and told to say that we had come to Honduras to join them, to make an appeal to the Nicaraguan people saying that we had left to join them and the rest should do likewise . . . And everything they told us to do we had to do, or else we would die."

The Barredas, too beaten to travel, stayed in the jail, while the other captives were taken to another camp.

"They said they had a camp where we were going to be taken, and whomever wanted could be trained in special commandos, specialized in torture, in interrogations and something like throat-cutting; they kept talking about special training, that they could send us to a training camp or to the United States or a place like that for classes . . . We were taken there at night forewarned of what would happen to us should we try to escape, which is what had happened to the three who had tried to escape a day earlier: a boy about thirteen years old, one of about seventeen and another of about twenty whose throats were cut right in front of us by a special commando that took care, they said of deserters. . . "

In June, 1983, when the Nicaraguan Government captured a young contra officer named Pedro Javier Nunez Cabezas, alias El Muerto ("the Dead Man"). Shown on national television, El Muerto was identified by Noel Benavides and the others as the man responsible for their maltreatment.

In statements given to the Nicaraguan press, El Muerto described the execution of the Barredas:

"At one-thirty, more or less, they brought Felipe Barreda, who had shrapnel wounds. Later at about five in the afternoon, they brought in senora Maria Eugenia who had been badly mistreated and had a bad vaginal hemorrage. I ordered that they be tied up (together with the four others) in a coffee plantation. The next day, the Barredas were brought blindfolded to a house to be interrogated. The interrogations were conducted separately. I applied psychological torture with the senora but I gave Mr. Barreda a blow on the head with the butt of my pistol and kicked him all over when he refused to accept what his wife had said . . .

During some sessions, we would only hit them in their

bodies, because we were waiting for the (counterrevolutionary television crew) and we didn't want them to appear with disfigured faces. Therefore the orders which I gave and executed were to kick them in the body, to hit them where it wouldn't leave any signs when the time came to show them on television . . .

That night they were both taken ouside nude so they would spend the night under the rain. The next day (the television) interviewed them. After that, El Suicida (El Muerto's superior) told me to kill the Barredas and I carried out the order shooting them in the head with the help of Juan and Tapir."

Conclusion

This report shows "that civilian casualties are apparently a primary objective of the contra strategy. What economic objective or military gain is there to be had in killing a five year old child, or in raping a grandmother, or slaughtering a young bride in front of her parents?," asks Congressman Gejdenson in a statement. "The only achievement is that of imposing a climate of total fear. And therein lies the contras' objective—to blanket the population in fear."

The Contras attack individuals deemed to be contributors to the country's economy or to its defense, explained the Law Group and WOLA in their statement, such as telephone workers, coffee pickers, teachers, technicians and members of the civilian-based militia. But substantial credible evidence exists that Contra violence is also directed at individuals who have no apparent economic, military or political significance.

HUMAN RIGHTS

THE NICARAGUAN DEMOCRATIC RESISTANCE

U.S. Department of State

The Department of State has prepared this resource paper on the Nicaraguan democratic opposition in response to requests from members of Congress, the press, and concerned citizens. Its purpose is to provide brief information on the principal opposition groups and their top leaders. The democratic opposition is frequently referred to as the "contras" by the Sandinistas and their supporters.

Points to Consider

1. Who are the resistance people and where do they come from?
2. Why are they fighting the Sandinistas?
3. What are the goals of the resistance?
4. How many organized groups now exist?

U.S. Department of State, "Groups of the Democratic Resistance: Who Are They?" *Resource Paper,* April, 1985, pp. 1-7.

65

The Sandinistas' opponents are indigenous Nicaraguans fighting for their cause. They are, as President Reagan said on February 11, "the people of Nicaragua who have been betrayed in the revolution that they themselves supported."

The Sandinista government of Nicaragua came to power in 1979, promising respect for pluralism and human rights, a non-aligned foreign policy, and a mixed economy. The communist leaders of the Sandinista National Liberation Front (FSLN) have consistently failed to honor these pledges made to the Organization of American States and the Nicaraguan people. They systematically pushed aside the democratic members of the broad-based coalition that overthrew Somoza . . .

It became clear to democratic Nicaraguan groups that the Sandinistas would not alter their behavior unless pressured from within and without.

Sandinista Repression

As a result of Sandinista repression and growing ties to communist countries, opposition developed, made up in part of persons who had been Sandinista supporters, even some who had been members of the post-revolutionary government, such as Alfonso Robelo, Arturo Cruz, Alfredo Cesar, and Eden Pastora, the legendary "Commander Zero." The Sandinistas' opponents are indigenous Nicaraguans fighting for their cause. They are, as President Reagan said on February 11, "the people of Nicaragua who have been betrayed in the revolution that they themselves supported."

There is, however, an obvious congruence between United States objectives and those of many of the anti-Sandinistas. United States objectives are clear:

—the reduction of Nicaragua's greatly expanded military apparatus to restore military equilibrium among the Central American nations;

—the removal of Soviet and Cuban military personnel and termination of their military and security involvement in Nicaragua;

—the termination of Nicaraguan support for subversion in neighboring countries; and

—the implementation of the Sandinistas' commitments to the OAS.

The Sandinistas are waging an intensive propaganda campaign to paint the opposition as henchmen of the former dictator Anastasio Somoza. But the facts show that nearly all of the opposition leaders (contras) opposed Somoza. This campaign, focused primarily on the Fuerza Democratica Nicaraguense (Nicaraguan Democratic Force, or FDN) which has a number of former National Guard officers in its membership, tries to equate former service in the National Guard with being a Somocista. But even if that questionable assumption were accepted, the number of former guardsmen in the FDN is relatively small. FDN records indicate that less than 2% of its members were guardsmen as compared to about 20% who are former Sandinistas.

Nicaraguan Resistance

Several groups of the armed and unarmed opposition met in San Jose, Costa Rica, and formed a coalition called the Nicaraguan Resistance. On March 2, 1985, they issued a document calling for a national dialogue with the Sandinistas under the sponsorship of the Nicaraguan Bishops' Conference. In addition to the dialogue, they called for:
— a cease-fire in place;
— lifting of the state of emergency;
— amnesty for political prisoners (approximately 3,500);
— granting the rights of habeas corpus and asylum;
— a guarantee of protection for participants in the dialogue.

The National Resistance offered to recognize Daniel Ortega as President pending a plebiscite. They called for the presence of guarantors from other Central America countries to oversee the proposed dialogue and invited other interested nations and groups to send observers. The opposition seeks only the right to participate in a free and open election and does not demand in advance, as do the Salvadoran leftist guerrillas, a place in the government . . .

The following descriptions of the principal opposition groups and their top leadership should help to counterbalance the misinformation being spread about them.

Principal Opposition Groups

The Nicaraguan Democratic Force, or *Fuerza Democratica Nicaraguense (FDN)*

The FDN, the largest of the armed opposition organizations, was founded in 1982. Although originally composed primarily of former guardsmen, as a focal point for armed resistance to the Sandinistas it quickly attracted many others who had become disaffected with the FSLN (*Frente Sandinista de Liberacion Nacional*). The influx of members led to a transformation of the FDN into a broadly based organization drawn from all sectors of Nicaraguan society.

The FDN's policy-making Directorate, reorganized in 1983, is composed of six persons. Five are civilians who were long-time opponents of Somoza; the other member is a former National Guard colonel, Enrique Bermudez, who heads the military general staff. The Directorate is responsible for making and carrying out all FDN policy.

The FDN reports that in 1982 a number of former Somoza National Guardsmen with records of human rights violations were expelled. Since that time, three FDN military leaders who had committed gross human rights violations were tried, found guilty, and executed under the leadership of the Directorate. A written policy requiring respect for human rights and good conduct is stressed constantly during the training and operations of the FDN soldiers . . .

The FDN reports that its overall military leadership, including the general staff and regional and task force commanders, has a greater number of former Sandinistas than National Guardsmen. The composition of the FDN military leadership is as follows:

Former Sandinistas	43%
Former National Guardsmen	32%
Campesinos (small farmers)	19%
Other	6%

Of the 56 regional and task force commanders in the FDN responsible for day-to-day operations, the FDN reports that 27 were former Sandinistas; 13 were National Guardsmen, none above the rank of lieutenant; and 12 were farmers. The remainder include a medical doctor, an evangelical minister, a fourth-year university student, and a civilian radio technician. The overwhelming number of the reported 15,000 FDN troops are peasants, workers, shopkeepers, businessmen, and others with no previous ties to Somoza.

The Democratic Revolutionary Alliance, or *Alianza Revolucionaria Democratica (ARDE)*

The Costa Rica-based ARDE is a coalition of organizations created in 1982 by individuals who were active during the revolution, including many who were initially officials in the Sandinista government. From its beginning, its leaders sought to restore the original course of the revolution through political means. In the spring of 1983, after peaceful efforts had proved futile, ARDE began military operations in southern Nicaragua. There have been internal disagreements among various ARDE leaders. In 1984, Eden Pastora, leader of the military arm, was expelled by other members of the ARDE coalition. There continues to be a dispute over which faction can legitimately claim the ARDE name, with both sides doing so. Pastora has retained the loyalty of most

ARDE troops and continues military operations in southern Nicaragua. The political head of ARDE, Alfonso Robelo, was a principal organizer of the Nicaraguan Resistance.

Current groups in the Robelo-led ARDE coalition are:

Nicaraguan Democratic Movement, or *Movimiento Democratico Nicaraguense (MDN)*

The MDN is a social-democratic party founded in 1978. It drew its support from lower and middle class Nicaraguans, including many peasants, and it played an active role in the revolution which overthrew Somoza. Its leader, Alfonso Robelo, was an original member of the ruling revolutionary junta. He resigned in protest over Sandinista efforts to create a communist state. Subjected to extraordinary harassment by the Sandinistas, Robelo went into exile in Costa Rica in 1982.

Nicaraguan Democratic Unity/Nicaraguan Revolutionary Armed Force, or *Unidad Democratica Nicaraguense/Fuerza Armada Revolucionaria Nicaraguense (UDN/FARN)*

UDN/FARN is a political/military organization founded by veteran anti-Somoza fighter Fernando "El Negro" Chamorro. UDN/FARN was one of the original founders of ARDE, but pulled out in 1983 in a policy dispute. In the spring of 1984 those differences were overcome and UDN/FARN rejoined the coalition. Chamorro was a signer of the Nicaraguan Resistance document.

MISURA

MISURA is an armed group that evolved out of an Atlantic Coast Indian organization ALPROMISO, founded in 1973 with the help of Protestant churches in that region, and its successor group MISURASATA. Former supporters of the Sandinista revolution, Miskito Indians Wycliffe Diego and Steadman Fagoth, founded MISURA in 1983. Its military operations are carried out in northeastern Nicaragua.

Nicaraguan Democratic Solidarity, or *Solidaridad de Trabajadores Democraticos Nicaraguense (STDN)*

STDN was founded in 1983 by two Nicaraguan labor leaders who had been forced into exile as a result of Sandinista persecution of the independent labor movement in Nicaragua. The founders had long been opponents of Somoza; one of them, Zacarias Hernandez, was a signer of the Nicaraguan Resistance document.

Independent Resistance Organizations

Sandino Revolutionary Front, or *Frente Revolucionario Sandino (FRS)*

The FRS was created in 1982 by disillusioned Sandinista militants, many of whom had fought on the southern front against Somoza in 1979. The FRS was a founding member of ARDE, but later its ties were severed. Its leader, Eden Pastora, has steadfastly refused to align himself or his organization with any former National Guardsmen. Most of ARDE's combat troops remain loyal to Pastora. In September 1984 the FRS entered into a new understanding with ARDE. However, Pastora has not signed the Nicaraguan Resistance document.

Miskito, Sumo, Rama, and Sandinista Unity, or *MISURASATA*

MISURASATA evolved out of the Atlantic Coast Indian organization ALPROMISO. Following the fall of Somoza, ALPROMISO was renamed MISURASATA. By the end of 1981, Sandinista persecution and the forced relocation of many Indian communities prompted the beginning of a large-scale exodus of Miskito Indians from Nicaragua, primarily to Honduras. The Nicaraguan government officially ordered MISURASATA disbanded, but members formed a fighting force to resist. It conducts military operations in southeastern and eastern Nicaragua. Divisions within the organization led to a split in 1982. Brooklyn Rivera heads the faction that retains the MISURASATA name. MISURASTA pulled out of ARDE in mid-1984 and was not a signer of the Nicaraguan Resistance document.

HUMAN RIGHTS

SANDINISTA REPRESSION IS A MYTH

Phillip Berryman

Phillip Berryman was Central America Representative for the American Friends Service Committee from 1976 to 1980. He is the author of The Religious Roots of Rebellion: Christians in Central American Revolutions *(Orbis Books, 1984).*

Points to Consider

1. How do many Latin Americans view Marxism?
2. What is "La Prensa" and how is it dealt with by the Sandinistas?
3. Why have accusations about large scale Sandinista human rights violations been found to be without evidence?
4. What is the role of the contras?

Phillip Berryman, "Illusions of Villany," *Sojourners,* August 14, 1984, pp. 13-17. Reprinted with permission of *Sojourners,* Box 29272, Washington, DC 20017.

International human rights commissions of both the Organization of American States and the United Nations have given Nicaragua generally high marks on human rights.

In order to win public opinion to its policies, the Reagan administration has sought to give a heroes-and-villains account of what is happening in Central America. Almost 40 percent of President Reagan's May 9, 1984 televised public address on his Central American policy was devoted to criticizing Nicaragua.

The Nicaraguan revolution is not faultless, but portraying it as "totalitarian" or "terrorist" runs directly counter to the experience of many Nicaraguan Christians and of many U.S. Christians who have visited Nicaragua. It appears that Nicaragua is the target of a propaganda campaign whose underlying purpose is to provide a rationale for a deepening U.S. intervention in Central America. What follow are responses to the most frequently heard statements of the propaganda campaign . . .

"Nicaragua is heading down the familiar road of Marxist totalitarianism."

Nicaraguans insist that their revolution is "Sandinista"—that is, it takes its inspiration from Augusto Cesar Sandino, the nationalist hero who withstood the U.S. Marine occupying force for five years. "Sandinismo" thus emphasizes the nationalistic side of the revolution, its aim to be Nicaraguan and not a copy of any other model.

For many Americans "Marxism" is an automatic put-down word; in Latin America, however, Marxist terminology and ideas are as pervasive as psychological jargon is in the United States. Many Latin Americans find that Marxism helps them analyze the roots of their society's problems and the need for structural change. The Sandinistas do not deny the element of Marxism in their policies, but they believe they can use it flexibly and non-dogmatically.

Just as the Sandinistas are seeking to work with a mixed economy, they propose political pluralism. What they have in mind is pluralism within the revolution. The aim is to encourage participation and criticism from those who support the overall direction of the Sandinista revolution.

Nicaragua might seem to be a one-party state, but so is Mexico. From the viewpoint of ordinary citizens, the key question is not so much whether parties compete in particular kinds of elections but whether their governments are responsive and whether they as citizens have a role in shaping policy.

Most Nicaraguans would not judge their government to be totalitarian.

"The press has been suppressed."

In the United States, *La Prensa* has often been portrayed as an independent paper, bravely resisting Sandinista harassment and censorship. This paper did play a major role in the anti-Somoza struggle. However, soon after Somoza's downfall, it began to take an anti-Sandinista line. At that point the bulk of its employees quit *La Prensa* and joined one of its owners in setting up *El Nuevo Diario*.

Many Nicaraguans view *La Prensa* as the voice of the anti-Sandinista elites and even as a tool to undermine the revolution. They see a clear historical precedent in the example of *El Mercurio* in Chile, which received CIA funding and was a major tool for the destabilization campaign that paved the way for the military overthrow of the elected Allende government. *La Prensa* seems to be following a similar model when it gives distorted reporting on food shortages, for example, and so creates a climate of insecurity. The overall line of *La Prensa* is similar to themes of the U.S. government: it creates the impression that Nicaragua is becoming a Soviet-aligned state and that the Sandinistas are hostile to religion; rarely does it find anything to praise in the revolution, and rarely, if ever, does it condemn the CIA-sponsored and -organized attacks on Nicaragua.

In dealing with *La Prensa,* the Sandinista government has tried to maintain a balance between safeguarding free expression on the one hand, and making sure that the revolution is not undermined. Its actions have become increasingly severe: *La Prensa* has been closed briefly, and pre-censorship has been imposed to prevent news coverage that might disrupt the country. Many Nicaraguans, very

74

I resent these unfounded accusations!

aware of what happened in Chile, agree that these measures are justified; others think that even under adverse conditions, the revolution would be better served by maintaining freedom of expression.

North Americans may be applying a double standard. One researcher found that of eight *New York Times* stories on the Nicaraguan elections scheduled for November 1984, six mentioned the issue of press freedom; and yet, of some 30 stories on the Salvadoran elections filed during the same period, the issue of press freedom was not broached, despite the fact that no opposition press is allowed in El Savador and journalists have been murdered there. In Guatemala approximately 50 journalists have been murdered, and many others have had to flee, with only minimal interest from the outside world.

"The Sandinista Government is repressive and violates human rights."

International human rights commissions of both the Organization of American States and the United Nations have given Nicaragua generally high marks on human rights. Contrary to what has happened after almost all revolutionary victories, no executions of members of the Somoza forces took place. The death penalty was abolished. Those National Guard members convicted of crimes were sentenced to prison; those judged innocent were set free.

Accusations of large-scale atrocities in Nicaragua, when examined, have been found to be without evidence. Human rights organizations such as Americas Watch have expressed concern about arbitrary arrest and detention of people for political reasons. In its report of April 1984, Americas Watch stated that the fate of about 70 Miskito Indians who disappeared in 1982 and some 28 non-Miskitos who disappeared in 1983 had not been clarified. The report points out that these disappearances took place in remote areas and that no case of such disappearances of Miskitos had occurred after 1982. If these people indeed disappeared in the hands of Sandinista forces, it is a severe human rights violation. However, the figure pales by comparison with Guatemala and El Savador, where tens of thousands have disappeared in recent years. Moreover, in Nicaragua some Sandinista soldiers have been brought to justice for human rights violations.

"The Sandinistas are seeking to destroy genocidally the Miskito culture and people."

Serious problems persist between the Sandinista government and the Miskitos. These are rooted in history, but they have been aggravated by Sandinista errors and exploited by the CIA. Indigenous people—Miskitos, Sumos, and Ramas—and the English-speaking blacks living on the Atlantic coastal plain make up about 4 percent of the Nicaraguan population. Their history has been quite separate from that of the rest of the country. They were colonized by Great Britain. They had little contact with the rest of Nicaragua and were mistrustful of the "Spaniards," as they call those from the Pacific side. The Atlantic side was largely untouched by the anti-Somoza struggle.

When the Sandinistas arrived in 1979, they inherited the existing mistrust of the "Spaniards," and their own insensitivity to the particular experience of the people increased that mistrust. In addition, the Miskitos were seeking autonomy in government, land rights, and the rights to natural resources on their lands.

Tensions increased, and events came to a head in February 1981 when the top leaders of the MISURASATA —the name means "Miskitos, Sumos, Ramas, Sandinistas, together—were arrested by the Sandinista authorities. They

A Sense of Freedom

What I saw, heard and felt in Nicaragua was very different from the litany coming from Washington. The Sandinista leaders admit they have made mistakes. There is a sense of freedom and openness generally in Nicaragua. I felt very comfortable walking the streets alone. The eagerness of the people to talk is unlike what I perceive to be true in repressive societies.

William D. Halverstadt, *The Minneapolis Tribune*, June 13, 1985

were soon released, but Steadman Fagoth, the indigenous representative on the Council of State, went to Honduras where he joined ex-Somoza guardsmen in counterrevolutionary activities. Eventually most of the other MISURASATA leaders also left Nicaragua and some became linked to anti-Sandinista groups.

In February 1982, in response to increasing attacks from Honduras, the Sandinistas decided to transfer inland the people living along the Honduran border. As they did so, they destroyed villages to prevent their being used by counterrevolutionary forces. Even those Miskitos who had experienced the cross-border attacks and agreed the transfer was necessary were saddened and angry. An estimated 18,000 Miskitos have left Nicaragua for Honduras out of a total Nicaraguan Miskito population of 80,000. Two thousand have been trained as combatants and are fighting the Sandinistas.

Since the CIA-organized and -financed *contras* would like to seize a portion of Nicaraguan territory, declare it "liberated," and then call for recognition from governments unfriendly to the Sandinista revolution, the "Miskito question" is inevitably part of the larger struggle going on in Nicaragua.

The Sandinistas publicly admit some errors and insensitivity to the indigenous people. Americas Watch, while reporting improvement in relations between the Sandinistas and the Miskitos, states that "serious problems remain."

"The Sandinistas have persecuted the churches and even organized mobs to insult the pope."

The churches find themselves divided over the revolution. Many grassroots pastoral workers see participation in the revolution as a practical consequence of their faith, and many lay church members agree. In addition to the well-known Christian participation of priests in the government, there are many Christian lay people who work with the revolution because they believe it offers the possibility of building a society more in accordance with the gospel. CEPAD, the umbrella organization of Protestant churches, works well with the Sandinista government in development projects.

However, most (but not all) of the Catholic bishops oppose

the Sandinista government, fearful that it will become a classic Marxist regime. In their outlook and views, these bishops are quite similar to the anti-Sandinista middle- and upper-class groups. Archbishop Obando y Bravo is the leading public figure opposing the government.

This situation offers many opportunities for anti-Sandinista groups, who would simply be rejected if they openly expressed their intention of rolling back the revolution. Religious language and symbols can serve as a code for counterrevolutionary groups.

Christians who support the revolution not only regret the use of Christian symbols to serve the counterrevolution, but they also fear that this behavior represents a tragic pastoral failure: the revolution offers the church opportunities for a new kind of evangelization, opportunities that will be missed if the church's leaders use their positions to undermine the revolution.

During March 1983, Pope John Paul II visited Nicaragua in this atmosphere of division. The Sandinista government declared a national holiday and provided bus transportation for all Nicaraguans to Managua (using more than two month's worth of fuel). During his Mass in Managua, the pope said nothing about the accomplishments of the revolution or about the attacks from outside, and showed no sympathy for the sorrow of families mourning the loss of 17 young people killed on the border a few days before. The people became impatient and, as is their custom, began to chant slogans, such as "We Want Peace!" The pope became visibly angry and shouted back "Silence!" three times. All evidence shows that the encounter was spontaneous.

"Nicaraguan 'freedom fighters,' including some former Sandinistas, are seeking to liberate Nicaragua from the Soviet-aligned *comandantes* who have usurped the revolution."

Since 1979 some former Somoza National Guardsmen have been based in camps in Honduras. In 1983 another group began operating out of Costa Rica. These groups have found some sympathizers and collaborators in the border regions, but their main support comes from the United States.

No revolt exists within Nicaragua. The upper and middle

classes are dissatisfied at the loss of their power. On the other hand, some of the poor are dissatisfied at what they see as the slowness of the revolution; for example, the Sandinistas have restrained peasant organizations from simply taking land. But support for the revolution remains strong.

The anti-Sandinista groups do not agree on what they propose for Nicaragua. The FDN (Nicaraguan Democratic Front) intends to reverse the Nicaraguan revolution by turning back land reform. Eden Pastora, the military leader of the ARDE (Democratic Revolutionary Alliance), claims his main objection to the Sandinistas is the Cuban influence in Nicaragua. The bulk of the CIA funding has gone to the FDN, but revelations of CIA funding for the ARDE forces as well further discredit Pastora, who is often touted as a hero of the anti-Somoza struggle. His popularity is overestimated in the United States.

By themselves, the anti-Sandinista groups cannot overthrow the Sandinista revolution, and they are incapable of igniting a revolt within Nicaragua, since most people there, whatever complaints they might have about the Sandinistas, recognize that a *contra* government could only be the most extreme sort of repressive dictatorship. *Contra* behavior (killing, raping, pillaging, destruction) indicates that any government those forces might form would be repressive. Hence, the people do not regard them as "freedom fighters" but as "Somocistas."

Implicitly recognizing that the *contras* were not successful, the CIA in the fall of 1983 moved toward conducting its own operations without Nicaraguan participation (bombing, sabotage, harbor mining).

If there is to be peace in Central America, the United States must recognize that the Nicaraguan revolution is a fact, and that the Sandinista government enjoys broad support among the majority of its people. The Nicaraguans have every reason to want to reach an accommodation with the United States, since their economy, history, and culture are tied to those of the West.

HUMAN RIGHTS

SANDINISTA
HUMAN RIGHTS VIOLATIONS

Country Report on Human Rights

*Country reports are submitted to the Congress by the
Department of State in compliance with Sections 116(d)(1)
and 502B(b) of the Foreign Assistance Act 1961, as amended.
The legislation requires reports on all countries which
receive aid from the United States, and all countries which
are members of the United Nations.*

Points to Consider

1. What promises have the Sandinistas failed to keep?
2. Who are the "contras"?
3. What oppressive methods have the Sandinistas used?
4. What two domestic human rights organizations operate in
   Nicaragua?

U.S. Department of State, *Country Reports on Human Rights Practices* for 1984, pp. 608-624.

*Government security forces reportedly
tortured and executed persons suspected
of assisting the guerrillas, while the
Government accused the guerrillas of killing and kidnapping civilians.*

A three-man junta—composed of one member of the
Sandinista National Directorate, another high-ranking
Sandinista member, and one pro-Sandinista Democratic
Conservative Party member—served as nominal head of the
Government of National Reconstruction throughout 1984.
The Junta was formally terminated following the January
1985 inauguration of President Daniel Ortega and Vice
President Sergio Ramirez, both former Junta members. Real
political power continued to be wielded by the National
Directorate of the Sandinista National Liberation Front, a
group of nine Marxist revolutionary leaders who took control
in July 1979. This body—of which the President is a
member—controls policy-making in the Government, and to
a large degree, implementation of policy through a parallel
party-government structure.

The Sandinistas seized power in 1979, forming a coalition
Government with broad popular support and promising to
replace the discredited Somoza dictatorship with new social,
political and economic systems based on the principles of
pluralism, free elections, a mixed economy, and observance
of human rights. In the ensuing five years, however, the
Government has not fulfilled these promises. It has used
intimidation and the restriction of basic human rights to
consolidate the power of the Sandinista Front. Though
elections were held on November 4, 1984, important sectors
of the political opposition declined to participate because of
the Government's failure to ensure conditions for a fair and
free campaign. Repression and intimidation by government
forces against the opposition political parties that did participate in the brief campaign further underscored the unfair
nature of the elections. . .

The Government continued in 1984 to support terrorist
groups in other countries of the region, notably in El
Salvador. Honduras and Costa Rica protested Nicaraguan

Army incursions and shellings of their territory. Throughout 1984, the Sandinista Government increasingly found itself fighting a civil war against anti-Sandinista guerrillas, which the Government called "counter-revolutionaries" or "contras" (terms used loosely by the Government to refer to guerrillas and anyone else it chooses to consider "subversive"). Government security forces reportedly tortured and executed persons suspected of assisting the guerrillas, while the Government accused the guerrillas of killing and kidnapping civilians. The Sandinista Army continued arbitrary and sometimes forced military conscription, prompting widespread dissatisfaction and several public protests by Nicaraguan mothers.

Sandinista Control

During 1984 the Government continued to tighten Sandinista control over Nicaraguan society and to intimidate the remaining opposition. The State of Emergency declared in 1982 remained in effect throughout 1984, although some provisions were modified. The Government continued to use Special Tribunals established outside the judicial system to try cases of suspected subversives. This denies the accused the better, though still flawed, legal protection provided by the regular courts. The Sandinistas continued to rely on organizations controlled by the Sandinista National Liberation Front, such as the ubiquitous "block committees," to

---

Sandinista Dictatorship

The Sandinistas no sooner came to power than they set about the progressive restriction of Nicaraguan rights, which had not been very extensive under Somoza in the first place. The media was immediately nationalized with the sole exception of La Prensa. The Sandinistas began at once to progressively restrict trade unions.

Jeane Kirkpatrick, *Transformation,* January, 1985

---

help implement their policies at the local level and to exert control, instill loyalty and to identify and implement sanctions against suspected opponents. Using both its own powers and intimidation by Sandinista organizations, the Government systematically harassed opposition political parties, independent labor confederations, the private sector, the Catholic Church, and the independent media. The Government continued prior censorship of the print and electronic media, and cracked down with new vigor in this area after some relaxation during the 1984 campaign period. Sandinista block committees and other organizations frequently disrupted campaign rallies held by opposition political parties, contravening guarantees in the electoral law. The police often did not intervene to prevent such harassment or violence. Through both legal and extra-legal means, the Government continued to seize private property. The 10,000 Miskito Indians forcibly resettled from their Rio Coco homelands in 1982 continued to be prohibited from returning there. About 2,000 more Miskitos fled en masse to Honduras in April and May. There are continuing credible reports that the security forces have tortured and killed Miskito Indians and have confiscated or destroyed their food supply and property.

Two domestic human rights organizations operate in Nicaragua. The Permanent Human Rights Commission (CPDH) is an independent agency established in 1977. It played a key role in exposing human rights violations committed under the new Government. Since 1981, the CPDH has been subject to constant harassment by the Sandinista National Liberation Front, impeding its work but not silencing its voice. . .

Political Killing

There is credible evidence that the military and security forces were responsible for the deaths of a number of detained persons in 1984. The CPDH documented six such cases, and it estimated that many more went unreported. The Government responded to these accusations by claiming some were "killed while attempting to escape" or "killed while resisting arrest," while others were allegedly guerrillas killed in combat. The CPDH also reported that military and police officials arbitrarily shot a number of suspected

DECEMBER 14, 1984 / NATIONAL REVIEW

subversives. In one case three officials reportedly shot a mentally handicapped farmer who they claimed was a dangerous suspect, though they had no warrant and did not present any charges to the family. Displaced persons reported that military and security forces operating in remote areas summarily executed local peasants whom they suspected were anti-government guerrillas or their sympathizers, sometimes after physically mutilating them. In the section on Nicaragua of its 1984 annual report, the Inter-American Human Rights Commission of the Organization of American States stated, "Concerning the right to live, human rights organizations have continued to denounce violations, especially in the forms of forced disappearances and as a result of the abuse of power by members of the security forces. The Commission has been able to verify that a large number of the denunciations referred to events that took place in the zones of conflict". . .

Disappearance

The security forces often hold suspected guerrillas and subversives incommunicado indefinitely without notifying family members. In 1984 the CPDH documented 60 cases of disappearances in which security forces were implicated, but in which the Government would not acknowledge involvement. In some of those cases, though reported in 1984, the individuals had actually disappeared in earlier years. The Government for its part claimed the guerrillas kidnapped many civilians. It is widely believed that many of these alleged kidnappings may have been voluntary desertions to the guerrillas. Anti-Sandinista guerrilla forces took captive three Sandinista Front members, including Sandinista National Assembly candidate Ray Hooker, on September 5. The guerrillas released all three on October 30 in exchange for three prisoners held by the Government. During 1984, one guerrilla group turned over 54 captured soldiers to the Costa Rican Red Cross.

Torture and Cruel, Inhuman or Degrading Treatment or Punishment

The CPDH continued to collect evidence of systematic physical and psychological abuse and torture. Prisoners were reportedly kept in cramped, dark cells and fed meals at irregular intervals in order to disorient them, ordered to use only their prison numbers and not their names, and subjected to physical abuse and to threats against their family. One prisoner claimed that food and medical attention were almost nonexistent, and that whatever supplemental foodstuffs were brought in through relatives were stolen by the guards. Another reported that he was kept naked in a cold cell with a ceiling so low he could not stand upright. Other reports alleged prisoners were suspended from the ceiling by their hands during interrogation. Prisoners also reported being beaten with chains, fists and gun butts. It was alleged that, as a form of punishment, one prisoner was placed in a cell with several tuberculoid prisoners. Cases of psychological torture were also frequently reported. Prisoners were forced to listen to the screams of those being tortured, then were told by security officials that the screams came from members of their families. One prisoner was told, falsely, that his family had been arrested by security officials, who forced the spouse to don prison garb. She and her husband were then allowed to see each other but not to converse. Reportedly, security officials physically abused and threatened alleged "subversives" and political suspects. Nicaraguans who fled to Costa Rica reported incidents of rape, torture and murder of children by security and military forces. In the case of Prudencio Baltadano, soldiers tied him to a tree and cut off his ears. Interior Minister Thomas Borge admitted that some cases of physical abuse and killings of detained persons by security forces had occurred, but claimed the Government was working to resolve the problem. The National Human Rights Commission also stated that occasional individual abuses of authority had occurred, but insisted that those guilty had been found and punished. . .

Denial of a Fair Public Trial

In April 1983 the Government established special "Popular Anti-Somocista Tribunals" to handle the rapidly growing number of cases of accused guerillas and "subversives." These tribunals, which became increasingly active, operate outside the conventional judicial system, and their decisions cannot be appealed to the regular court system. The members of the tribunals are selected from the ranks of Sandinista organizations, and only the president of each tribunal is required to be a lawyer. Persons tried in these courts have the right to counsel and to introduce evidence, but the tribunals are granted great discretionary powers in determining whether evidence is admissible and whether it is sufficient for conviction. The proceedings of the tribunals are declared to be open to the public, but in some cases attendance is restricted. . .In its 1984 annual report, the Inter-American Human Rights Commission wrote that, "The procedures followed by the Anti-Somoza Courts give rise to serious doubts with respect to observance of the norms that gurarantee due process."

HUMAN RIGHTS

INDIAN RESISTANCE
IN NICARAGUA

Bernard Nietschmann

*Bernard Nietschmann is Professor of Geography at the
University of California, Berkeley and has written three
books on the Indians of eastern Nicaragua based on
research carried out over the last 15 years. He is now working on a book about the Indian-Sandinista war.*

Points to Consider

1. Why are the Indians fighting the Sandinistas?
2. What are the various Indian organizations and what are
   their goals?
3. How are the Indians exploited by all factions?
4. What could the Sandinistas do to stop the Indian
   resistance against them?
5. What is meant by the term "Fourth World"?

Bernard Nietschmann, "The Indian Resistance in Nicaragua,"
Akwesasne Notes, Spring, 1984, pp. 12, 13.

"We are not fighting for democracy — we never had it from any government. We are fighting for something that was taken away from us. We are fighting for our land. For an Indian freedom is land, not democracy."

Eastern Nicaragua's Miskito, Sumo and Rama Indian situation is complex and has attracted wide-ranging and contrasting explanations. In January I visited Indians in refugee camps in Costa Rica and Indians inside Nicaragua who are fighting against the Sandinista government. This was my third "unofficial" trip inside Nicaragua since mid-1983 with representatives of the Indian organization MISURASATA to talk with villagers and Indian military leaders in order to learn firsthand their views on their struggle. The Indian perspective on the Indian resistance is seldom sought and almost totally absent from discussions of the Indian-Sandinista conflict. I would like to share here the rationale and goals of the Indians who are actively resisting, politically and militarily, the FSLN (Frente Sandinista de Liberacion Nacional), and to place these within the context of other interpretations that are often given by the media, the United States, the Sandinistas, and the Indians' supposed allies, the FDN (Fuerza Democratica Nicaraguense) and ARDE (Alianza Revolucionaria Democratica).

The Resistance

Miskito, Sumo and Rama Indians have been fighting against the Nicaraguan government for three years. The Indians were the first to militarily oppose the FSLN, beginning in February 1981 (a year before the FDN and two years before ARDE). The resistance is widespread, longterm, determined, and operates throughout Indian territory in eastern Nicaragua and from border areas near Costa Rica and in Honduras. The Indians call it an Indian revolution and do not see themselves as *contras* (counterrevolutionaries), but as Indian revolutionaries fighting for Indian objectives. To be sure, their struggle is in many ways part of the overall anti-Sandinista war, but their reasons and goals are not. They say

89

they are fighting to establish their rights for self-determination, to regain their traditional lands, and for autonomy. They are fighting for Indian control of Indian territory, not to overthrow the Sandinista government or to make it more democratic. As one Indian leader told me: "The *contra* groups like the FDN and ARDE are fighting for democracy and representative free elections. We are fighting for something else. We are not fighting for democracy—we never had it from any government. We are fighting for something that was taken away from us. We are fighting for our land. For an Indian freedom is land, not democracy."

Revolution and Justice

"The revolution cannot succeed or survive in Nicaragua if there is not justice for the Indian people."

Brooklyn Rivera, Seattle, Washington speech, 1985.

From the Indians' perspective, all governments in the Americas are anti-Indian. Indians are dying in Guatemala and in Nicaragua. Right wing, left wing, military junta, democratic, Marxist, or whatever, Indian lands and cultures everywhere are under attack by the state. However, these Indians have made the decision to resist rather than passively accept decisions forced upon them . . .

During the twentieth century dictatorships, the Miskito, Sumo and Rama maintained effective control over their village communal lands and resources, but government leases given to foreign companies bypassed Indian determination over land and natural resource use in many areas of their territory. After 1979, FSLN agarian reform aimed to expropriate under state control land deemed to be underused or misused. Because Indians practice ecologically adapted long fallow agriculture, their land use system is dependent on having large amounts of land in fallow and small amounts under cultivation at any one time. Forest reserves, pasture land and surplus land for future population growth are integral parts of each community's territory. What the FSLN saw as surplus land was transferred to state control for eventual development and redistribution. The Indians saw this as outright theft of their lands backed up by a massive military presence, and foreign advisors. The FSLN believed that the revolution gave them the right to "integrate" Indian lands and peoples into Nicaragua; the Indians saw that the revolution gave the FSLN the power but not the rights to do so. The rights to decisions over Indian land and peoples were Indian rights.

The Indians seek to maintain communal ownership of their village lands which collectively comprise Indian nations and to continue their primary allegiance to those nations as distinct peoples. The FSLN seeks to incorporate what they see to be ethnic minorities into the revolution as citizens whose allegiance is to the revolution and whose territories are to be brought under national sovereignty . . .

Fourth World Wars

Because the Indians' limited goals do not fit into the two-dimensional "right vs. left" geopolitical and media analyses of the Nicaraguan conflict, they are made to fit. At the international level the Indian resistance is usually referred to paternalistically as "U.S.-backed disaffected Indian contras," as if the Indians were not fighting for their own reasons (the equivalent of "French-backed disaffected colonists" to describe the forces that opposed the British during the American Revolution). The United States uses the violations of Indians' human rights just to discredit the Sandinista government, conveniently ignoring what the Indians are fighting for and focusing only on what has happened to them. A strong pro-indigenous stance is hardly part of U.S. domestic or international policy. The FSLN, while maintaining that the Indian opposition is externally provoked and manipulated as part of CIA-directed destabilization efforts, recently has admitted mistakes and errors in their Indian policies and has released many Indian political prisoners and announced a general ill-defined amnesty that is to date unattractive and being ignored by Indians fighting, in exile, and in refugee camps. (Although the amnesty is an important first step toward potential political negotiations, the Indians do not see there is anything to come home to. In fact, since

the December '83 amnesty, Indians have continued to flee
from Nicaragua. To counter this embarrassment, ARDE and
the FDN have been falsely accused by members of the
Nicaraguan government of prohibiting Indian refugees from
leaving Costa Rica and Honduras.) And the Indians' military
allies—the FDN and ARDE—are wary and unsupportive of Indian goals of autonomous control over Indian territory,
resources and peoples. In the face of the still unresponsive
Sandinista government, the Indian resistance has to continue these alliances to obtain weapons and logistical aid for
their own objectives, realizing full well that their tenuous
allies are limiting and marginalizing support so as to reduce
their military potential to small-scale guerrilla activities and
to nullify their political potential so that they do not become
a well-armed army of Indian nationalists that would oppose
any new government that did not grant them their land and
rights. Even if the current Nicaraguan conflict was to be
"solved" politically or militarily, if the Indians don't regain
their land and achieve self-determination, they will continue
to fight. In the midst of this struggle,they actively discuss
and plan for what unfortunately may be the next war, Indian
vs. non-Indians, eastern Nicaragua vs. western Nicaragua . . .

Miskito warrior leader inside Nicaragua.
Photo by Bernard Nietschmann

FSLN Oppression

What they see as FSLN oppression has served as a catalyst for political and military resistance. This is the situation inside Nicaragua that continues to fuel their determination to fight on despite the odds: 1) one-fourth of the coast's 165,000 Indians are in military-controlled "relocation camps," or are in refugee camps in Honduras or Costa Rica; 2) one-half of Miskito and Sumo villages have been destroyed; 3) Indian rights to self-government, traditional land and resources have been abolished; 4) subsistence cultivation, fishing and hunting are strictly controlled, and access to staple foods is so limited that hunger is an everyday problem and starvation a real probability in many communities; 5) many villages have had no medicine or doctors for over two years; 6) freedom of movement is denied or severely restricted; 7) more than 35 Indian communities have suffered massive Sandinista military invasions during which civilians have been arbitrarily arrested, interrogated, tortured, killed, raped, personal belongings stolen, and livestock and crops destroyed in an unsuccessful effort to force the villagers to divulge the location of the Indian warrior's secret base camps and to terrorize the villagers so that they won't support or join the warriors. As bad as it was under the Somoza dictatorships, the Indians have suffered much more in the 4½ years of the Sandinistas than they did during the 43 years of the Somozas.

During their three years of armed resistance to the FSLN, the Indians have not lost a military confrontation . . .

The Sandinista military solution to control the Indians has not worked. After several years of fighting the Indians it should be evident to them that they cannot defeat the Indians' guerrilla forces that are permanently established and supported inside Nicaraguan Indian territory. Furthermore, so-called Indian "leaders" working with the Managua government do not represent Indian interests or the vast majority of Indian non-combatants, certainly not the Indians fighting. While these "leaders" may be important to the FSLN for seeking international support of their Indian policies, they do not represent a viable solution for the actual domestic conflict . . .

Four Possibilities

Based on my discussions with Indian political and military leaders about the course of their struggle, I want to present four hypothetical situations of varying probabilities for future Indian actions:

1. The Indians could continue as they are, underarmed and undersupported by their allies and simply try to wear down the Sandinistas militarily and economically until it is too costly for the FSLN, and some sort of resolution is achieved, either independently of the FDN and ARDE position, or part of it.

2. The Indians' FDN and ARDE allies could take a strong, pro-Indian position, sign and support treaties for Indian control of Indian land, and provide greater logistical and arms support to help the Indians push the Sandinistas from eastern Nicaragua. The Indians have a potential force of 10,000 warriors and they represent the quickest way to massively expand military pressure on the FSLN.

3. Another outside interest could step in and provide arms and logistical support to the Indians as a means to establish a political beachhead in the Americas; China, for example.

4. Or, the FSLN could evolve a much-needed pro-Indian policy, recognizing that Indian land and self-determination aspirations are not "counter-revolutionary," and begin negotiations with authentic Indian leaders with the goal of adapting some of the revolution to the Indians, not just the Indians to the revolution. If the FSLN were to guarantee Indian-control of traditional Indian land, help rebuild the destroyed villages, and arm the Indians, they would solve a military problem, isolate FDN and ARDE forces by breaking the connecting guerrilla link in eastern Nicaragua, allow the Indians to defend their territory from *contra* incursions, and thus be able to concentrate their FSLN forces on the northern and southern borders.

Of the three anti-Sandinista wars—the FDN, ARDE, and the Indians—the Indian conflict would be for the FSLN the easiest to resolve. On the other hand, it is also the one that would be the easiest to suddenly expand. These options to shut down or open up Indian resistance will be accepted by the Indians to the extent that they see the possibilities to achieve their goals of self-determination and Indian control of Indian land.

INDIAN AUTONOMY
IN NICARAGUA

Jose G. Perez

Jose G. Perez is a correspondent and columnist for **The Mili-**
tant *in Nicaragua. In this article, he describes new efforts by
the Sandinistas to bring about peaceful relations with Atlantic Coast Indians in Nicaragua.*

Points to Consider

1. What is the Atlantic Coast region and who lives there?
2. Describe conditions for this region under Somoza.
3. What kind of autonomy plan is being presented to the Indians?

"Jose G. Perez, "Nicaragua Discusses Atlantic Coast Autonomy,"
The Militant, August 2, 1985, pp. 8,9.

Autonomy does not mean the breakup of the Nicaraguan nation: Autonomy means, among other things, that we recognized the multilingual, multiethnic, multicultural character of the nation.

The Nicaraguan people are beginning a nationwide discussion on establishing local government autonomy for the Atlantic Coast region of the country, where most Nicaraguan Indians and Blacks live.

The Atlantic Coast region comprises roughly half of Nicaraguan territory. Out of Nicaragua's population of more than 3 million, about 230,000 live on the Atlantic Coast. Seventy thousand of them are Miskito Indians, another 8,000 Sumo Indians, and a small number are Rama Indians, each with their own language. Most of the 30,000 Blacks on the Coast are Creoles, many of whom speak English as well as Spanish, and a small number are Garifonos, speaking a dialect known as Gari.

Spanish-speaking Nicaraguans are the majority on the Pacific Coast and in the country as a whole. A good number of Spanish-speaking Nicaraguans also live on the Atlantic side of the country.

Historic Reality of Coast

The Atlantic Coast Indians and Blacks have languages, traditions and cultures different from that of the Spanish-speaking majority in Nicaragua. Historically, the Coast peoples have suffered not only from oppression as Nicaraguans, but also specific forms of racial discrimination as Miskitos, Sumos, Ramas, Creoles, or Garifonos.

Under the Somoza dictatorship, the Atlantic Coast was a paradise for U.S. and Canadian companies. They stripped the region of much of its resources, and kept it isolated from and far less developed than the Pacific side of the country.

In 1979 a popular insurrection of workers and peasants, based on the Pacific side of the country, overthrew the Somoza tyranny. This opened the door to overcoming the isolation and economic backwardness of the Atlantic Coast and uprooting the specific forms of oppression suffered by its peoples, and unifying the nation.

The autonomy proposal has grown out of the revolution's six years of experience in striving to meet these goals... Daniel Ortega, Nicaragua's president, traced the history of the Atlantic Coast under the Somoza regime and the changes brought about when Nicaragua's workers and peasants overthrew the dictatorship and established their own government.

Under Somoza, the resources of the Atlantic Coast—wood, gold, fish and bananas—were freely plundered by U.S. and Canadian companies. "The U.S. officials who supported Somoza and the U.S. and Canadian companies that exploited those territories had no concern for the situation and living conditions of the inhabitants of the Atlantic Coast," Ortega explained.

They "exploited not only the Atlantic Coast's forests, not only its subsoil, not only its mineral resources, but also, its inhabitants."

Effects of War

After the revolution triumphed, he continued, the new government nationalized the gold mines and began taking steps to rehabilitate the mining areas. The government began health projects on the Coast, expanded transportation, and made more resources available. It began development projects in fishing and reforestation.

FSLN members from the Pacific Coast came to the Atlantic to help carry out these projects. They arrived with "very good will and spirit," said Ortega. But lacking knowledge of the area and the traditions and cultures of its peoples, they made errors. Just as the FSLN was beginning to overcome these errors, he explained, the U.S. government-sponsored *contras* (counterrevolutionaries) began their war against Nicaragua.

The Atlantic Coast was one of the main targets of the mercenaries' war. They unleashed terror against the Coast's Indians and Blacks, and at the same time tried to convince them that the revolutionary government would destroy their traditional culture, languages, and national rights. A significant number of Miskito peasants in particular were convinced or coerced into joining the counterrevolutionary forces.

The war exacerbated the difficulties for the revolutionary government on the Coast. "When you have a war, tensions increase...errors are made, and excesses occur," Ortega explained. The policies of the FSLN and the government were not always applied in the best manner, he said.

But today, he continued, because of the revolution and despite the ongoing war, Nicaragua is ready to establish local government autonomy on the Coast.

The FSLN leaders have made clear from the beginning that autonomy does not mean independence or separation of the Atlantic Coast from Nicaragua, which they oppose.

Ortega explained the difference by contrasting the Sandinista view of autonomy to the promise of "autonomy" that the U.S. government has held out to the Coast peoples, particularly the Miskitos. Claiming to support Indian rights, Washington has appealed to the Miskitos to take up arms against the revolution and separate from Nicaragua. "The autonomy proposed by the U.S. government and its CIA agents...is nothing but the negation of autonomy for the Nicaraguan people," Ortega explained. It would lead not to liberation, but to the reimposition of U.S. domination. He pointed to Washington's record on the rights of U.S. Indians.

"Reagan is trying to cut in half our rivers, our mountain ranges, our valleys. He's trying to cut apart our country in order to dominate us."

Oppression and Poverty

Today, thousands of Miskitos suffer from lung disease, malnutrition and other poverty-related illnesses.

The Sandinista government is trying to change this pattern of oppression and neglect, combining health, education and social service programs with an ambitious reforestation project, new industry and increased cultivation of basic grains.

Beth Stephens & Maggi Pepkin, *In These Times,* January 11-17, 1984

"But this will not be possible, because here we are reuniting the Atlantic with the Pacific," he explained.

"The autonomy defended by the revolution," Ortega said, "is one of recognizing historic rights, recognizing values, recognizing realities; but above all it is for uniting, integrating, and definitively and forever joining together the Nicaraguans who live on the Atlantic Coast with those who live on the Pacific."

The main points of the autonomy plan were outlined in a speech by Minister of the Interior Tomas Borge. He delivered his speech partly in Miskito, Sumo, and English, as well as in Spanish.

Three Aspects of Autonomy

Borge explained that the autonomy plan is based on three pillars: "guarantee of effective exercise of autonomous rights by the inhabitants of the Atlantic Coast; the indivisible unity of the Nicaraguan nation; and the anti-imperialist, popular, and democratic principles of the Sandinista People's Revolution.

"When we speak of autonomy," Borge explained, "we speak of an autonomy that negates oppression, that negates the marginalization of the Indians and ethnic communities of the Coast, that recognizes with realism and respect the existence of their languages, of their customs, of their forms of organization, of their economic relations."

At the same time, Borge explained, autonomy is based on the common denominators of the various groups, "the principal one being Nicaragua's nationality." Autonomy, he stressed, does not mean the breakup of the Nicaraguan nation: "The Nicaraguan nation is one, and indivisible."

"Autonomy means, among other things, that we recognized the multilingual, multiethnic, multicultural character of the nation...

"A revolution inevitably has to recognize these rights so that it could be a revolution," he said.

'An Economist Approach'

Borge also explained the evolution of the FSLN's policy toward the Atlantic Coast.

The FSLN's 1969 program, he noted, recognized "the

legitimate aspirations of the inhabitants of the Coast." In 1981, after the revolution had triumphed, the FSLN National Directorate issued a declaration of principles recognizing the right of the Coast peoples to form their own organizations, to learn to read and write their own languages, to hold communal lands and property, and to be represented in the Nicaraguan Council of State.

But the revolutionary government did not initially see the importance of the autonomy question, Borge explained. "At first, we chose an economist approach," he said. We thought that in order to satisfy the historic demands of the Coast, it was enough to solve the problems of underdevelopment. We tended to differentiate rather than to unite; we did not make the inhabitants of the Coast equal participants in the projects launched by the national state. Our vision, as Daniel pointed out, was limited. We were not knowledgeable about the formation and the dynamics of the different social groups. The old ethnocentrist habits and the inadequacy of our program exacerbated the regionalism of the Coast itself."

Borge appealed to all Nicaraguans—whether from the Atlantic or the Pacific—to learn about and develop respect for each other's history and traditions. "Let us stop repeating the echo of chauvanist and ethnocentric positions that were stimulated by the sad, clumsy, and obscene oligarchy that has always ruled Nicaragua."

At the same time, Borge said, "Let the Atlantic, for its part, continue demanding its rights: the right to defend their traditional forms of social organization; the right to possess and use their lands; the right to participate in the decisions that affect their lives."

Legitimacy of Demands

"The essence of autonomy is the recognition of the legitimacy of these demands," he said.

"These demands are a part of the Sandinista People's Revolution to affirm its popular, democratic, and anti-imperialist character," he explained. "Moreover, only in the framework of the revolution can the ethnic question be solved."

Borge contrasted Nicaragua's proposed autonomy plan to the policy followed toward Indian peoples by other governments of the Americas.

Some governments, he said, have thought "that the Indian problem is the problem of lack of development." They have carried out a policy aimed at "integrating" the native peoples, "assuming that economic transformations will solve the problem.

"And hasn't it been demonstrated in practice that this integrationism, instead of solving the problems, only makes them worse?...Don't they make them worse by trying to resolve long-preserved ethnic and cultural characteristics of these peoples?"

Against Reservations

At the same time, Borge continued, other nations have proposed "recognizing a territory over which the indigenous group exercises sovereignty.

"But this solution reminds us of the Indian reservations and history has shown that such reservations have never permitted the development of the Indian communities. On the contrary, North American Indians were caged in these reservations.

"We vehemently reject the theory and practice of Indian reservations."

Nicaragua's decision to grant autonomy, Borge explained, "is an example not only for Latin America, but for all peoples of the world."

WHAT IS EDITORIAL BIAS?

This activity may be used as an individualized study guide for students in libraries and resource centers or as a discussion catalyst in small group and classroom discussions.

The capacity to recognize an author's point of view is an essential reading skill. The skill to read with insight and understanding involves the ability to detect different kinds of opinions or bias. Sex bias, race bias, ethnocentric bias, political bias and religious bias are five basic kinds of opinions expressed in editorials and all literature that attempts to persuade. They are briefly defined in the glossary below.

Glossary of Terms for Reading Skills

sex bias— *the expression of dislike for and/or feeling of superiority over the opposite sex or a particular sexual minority*

race bias— *the expression of dislike for and/or feeling of superiority over a racial group*

ethnocentric bias—the expression of a belief that one's own group, race, religion, culture or nation is superior. Ethnocentric persons judge others by their own standards and values.

political bias—the expression of political opinions and attitudes about domestic or foreign affairs

religious bias—the expression of a religious belief or attitude

Guidelines

1. From the readings in chapter three, locate five sentences that provide examples of editorial opinion or bias.

2. Write down each of the above sentences and determine what kind of bias each sentence represents. Is it sex bias, race bias, ethnocentric bias, political bias or religious bias?

3. Make up one sentence statements that would be an example of each of the following: *sex bias, race bias, ethnocentric bias, political bias* and *religious bias.*

4. See if you can locate five sentences that are factual statements from the readings in chapter three.

5. What is the editorial message of the cartoon captioned "Nicaragua" by Susan Harlan?

By Susan Harlan, USA TODAY

CHAPTER 4

THE SANDINISTAS AND U.S. POLICY

SANDINISTAS
AND U.S. POLICY

THE WORLD COURT
AND NICARAGUA'S LAWSUIT:
THE POINT

Central America Alert

The following comments were taken from Central America
Alert, *a publication of a non-profit organization called U.S.
Out of Central America, 2940 16th Street, Suite 7, San Fran-
sisco, CA 94103.*

Points to Consider

1. Why did the Nicaraguan government file suit against the
   United States in the World Court?
2. How did the U.S. respond to this lawsuit?
3. How is U.S. policy toward Nicaragua described?

"This article is reprinted with permission from *Central America Alert*
Vol. II, No. 3, May 1984. Published by U.S. Out of Central America,
2940 16th Street, San Fransisco, CA 94103.

The escalating aggressions of the administration's undeclared war against Nicaragua menace world peace.

Faced with growing domestic and international opposition to his Central American policies, Ronald Reagan is responding with increasing arrogance, belligerence, and defiance of all law. In recent weeks, the Reagan administration has been brought before the World Court of the United Nations on multiple charges of international law violations and has flagrantly usurped the authority of the U.S. Congress.

First the Nicaraguan government filed suit against the United States in the World Court, charging the Reagan administration with "using military force against Nicaragua...in violation of...the most fundamental and universally-accepted principles of international law."

Nicaragua's suit was followed by U.S. congressional outrage at Reagan's actions. Thirteen members of the House Judiciary Committee called for the appointment of a special prosecutor to look into Reagan's support of the military attacks on Nicaragua, which the Representatives say "appear to violate" the Neutrality Act and "strike at heart of the Congressional power to declare war." Likewise, Senator Edward Kennedy has charged that "There is no justification whatever for the administration to defy the Constitution and laws of the United States by permitting the escalation of similar combat activities by U.S. forces in El Salvador and Honduras."

The escalating aggressions of the administration's undeclared war against Nicaragua menace world peace, while Reagan's bid for near-dictatorial powers over U.S. foreign policy clearly threatens basic principles of the U.S. Constitution. Following are 12 examples of Reagan's lawless and authoritarian behavior.

International Violations

1. By refusing to submit to the jurisdiction of the World Court of the United Nations in the suit brought against Nicaragua, the Reagan administration is breaking a 1946 Presidential declaration signed by President Truman in

accordance with a U.S. Senate resolution. That declaration recognized with certain qualifications the jurisdiction of the World Court concerning, among other issues, "any question of international law," and stated that 6 months' prior notice must be given in order to terminate the agreement.

2. Through its mining of Nicaraguan harbors and its creation of a mercenary army of over 10,000 to be directed against the government of Nicaragua, the Reagan administration is in violation of the Charter of the United Nations, which states: "All members shall refrain in their international relations from the threat or use of force against the territorial integrity or political independence of any State."

Aggression Against Nicaragua

Jan. 18, President Reagan announced that the U.S. government will refuse to take part in any further World Court proceedings in connection with Nicaragua's lawsuit against the United States because of U.S. mining of the harbors of Nicaragua's two principal ports.

May 10, 1984, the court at the Hague ordered the United States to cease the mining. Nov. 26, 1984, by a 15-1 vote, the International Court of Justice (ICJ) ruled that it had jurisdiction to rule on Nicaragua's suit for damages for the explosions in which eight Nicaraguan fishermen died and nine ships from five nations were damaged.

The U.S. government's decision to walk away from the court is a boycott unprecedented in American history. . .

The United States, in other words, is not going to tell the one court in the world set up for lawsuits between nations about its clandestine, unilateral aggression against Nicaragua.

Robert F. Drinan, *National Catholic Reporter,* 1985

3. Through acts of military aggression and economic destabilization, recognized by members of the U.S. Congress as intended to overthrow the government of Nicaragua, the Reagan administration is in violation of the Charter of the Organization of American States, which declares: "No State or group of States has the right to intervene, directly or indirectly, for any reason whatsoever, in the internal or external affairs of any other state."

4. The CIA's mining of Nicaraguan harbors is not only in violation of the U.N. Charter, but also is a breach of the international Convention Relative to the Laying of Automatic Submarine Contact Mines, to which both Nicaragua and the United States are parties.

5. The Reagan administration's actions against Nicaragua are in violation of the Neutrality Act, which makes it a criminal offense to furnish money for or prepare for a military enterprise against a country at peace with the United States.

Ignoring the U.S. Congress and Constitution

6. Only the U.S. Congress has the power to declare war, and it has not declared war against Nicaragua. Yet the CIA, with authorization of the Reagan administration, has in fact been waging open warfare against the government of Nicaragua. This is in violation of the U.S. Constitution. Even Ronald Reagan has admitted that the Vietnam War should have been formally declared.

7. The Reagan administration is likely in violation of the U.S. War Powers Act, according to House Speaker Tip O'Neill, for not reporting to Congress on the use of American pilots in combat support missions in El Salvador. The 1973 War Powers Act requires the President to notify Congress within 48 hours of the onset of "imminent involvement in hostilities" by U.S. troops.

8. Despite restrictions prohibiting U.S. advisors in El Salvador from even working in areas where combat is likely to occur, in fact American advisors have accompanied Salvadoran pilots while they have engaged in combat and bombed guerilla positions.

9. According to Francis A. Boyle, a professor of international law at the University of Illinois, by unilaterally refusing to recognize the jurisdiction of the U.N. World Court, initially

agreed upon by a declaration of the U.S. Senate in 1946, the Reagan administration in effect is violating the Constitutional right of the U.S. Senate to give its advice and consent on all treaties. Reagan is thus further usurping powers that do not in fact belong to the President.

10. In violation of the U.S. Intelligence Oversight Act of 1980, which says that intelligence committees of Congress will be kept "fully and currently informed of all intelligence

activites," the CIA delayed for six weeks in responding to a request by the Senate Select Committee on Intelligence for a briefing on covert activities in Nicaragua, which included the mining of harbors.

In protest of this violation, Senator Barry Goldwater fired off an angry letter to CIA Director William Casey, stating: "[M]ine the harbors in Nicaragua? This is an act violating international law. It is an act of war. For the life of me, I don't see how we are going to explain it."

Outrage in Congress was such that even the Republican-controlled Senate, like the House, by an overwhelming majority passed a nonbinding resolution denouncing Reagan's policy of mining the harbors in Nicaragua.

11. House Democratic leaders have charged that the Reagan administration is illegally using unauthorized funds for the improvement and construction of military installations in Honduras, as part of the U.S. military build-up in that country.

12. Despite the fact that Congress has not approved the President's aid requests for El Salvador, Reagan has ordered $32 million in emergency arms shipments to El Salvador. In doing so, Reagan is at best stretching the law of Congressional control over appropriations. In response to Reagan's action, Senator Gary Hart, in an interview with the *Alert,* stated that "Congress will not allow President Reagan to sidestep our Constitutional authority on matters of war and peace."

These actions add up to an administration operating increasingly outside the laws of the nation and the world and in complete disdain of the authority of institutions created to oversight or mediate international relations. In a world bristling with nuclear weapons and strained to the breaking point by international tensions, the lawless, uncontrolled military aggressions of the Reagan administration could pitch us headlong into global annihilation. Reagan must be brought under control.

SANDINISTAS AND U.S. POLICY

THE WORLD COURT AND NICARAGUA'S LAWSUIT: THE COUNTERPOINT

Davis R. Robinson

Davis R. Robinson is the legal advisor of the Department of State. The following comments are excerpted from an oral argument he made before the World Court in the Hague.

Points to Consider

1. What examples of Nicaraguan aggression are given?
2. What are the Contadora negotiations?
3. How do Nicaragua's claims before the World Court undermine the peace process?

Davis R. Robinson, "U.S. Argument Against Nicaraguan Claim," *Department of State Bulletin,* January, 1985, pp. 24-29.

111

The U.S. Congress made an explicit statutory finding that Nicaragua was "providing military support (including arms, training, and logistical, command and control facilities) to groups seeking to overthrow the Government of El Salvador and other Central American Governments."

It is an honor to argue once again in 1984 before the International Court of Justice (ICJ) in the representation of my country. The United States maintains now, as it did in April, that this court is manifestly without jurisdiction over Nicaragua's claims. By appearing again to argue this conviction, the United States reaffirms its commitment to the rule of law in international relations and its faith and expectation that this Court will rule on the issues presently before it in accordance with that law . . .

It may be noted that, in December 1983, the U.S. Congress made an explicit statutory finding that Nicaragua was "providing military support (including arms, training, and logistical, command and control facilities) to groups seeking to overthrow the Government of El Salvador and other Central American Governments . . ." More detailed findings with respect to Nicaragua's aggression against its neighbors may be found in a May 1983 report to the Permanent Select Committee on Intelligence of the U.S. House of Representatives, which is quoted at page 77 of the U.S. Countermemorial.

The states of Central America confirm the conclusions of the United States in this regard and have so informed this Court. The Government of the Republic of El Salvador, for example, stated in its 15 August 1984 Declaration of Intervention:

El Salvador considers itself under the pressure of an effective armed attack on the part of Nicaragua and feels threatened in its territorial integrity, in its sovereignty, and in its independence, along with the other Central American countries . . .El Salvador comes here to affirm before the International Court of Justice and before the entire world, the aggression of which it is a victim through subversion that is directed by Nicaragua, and that endangers the stability of the entire region.

The representative of Honduras stated to the Security Council in April of this year—a few days before Nicaragua's application was filed:

My country is the object of aggression made manifest through a number of incidents by Nicaragua against our territorial integrity and civilian population. Those elements which have obliged (Honduras) to strengthen its defenses are mainly the disproportionate amount of arms in Nicaragua, the constant harassment along our borders, the promotion of guerrilla groups which seek to undermine our democratic institutions, and the warmongering attitude of the Sandinist commanders.

To the same effect, the Government of Costa Rica has repeatedly made diplomatic representations to Nicaragua protesting "attack(s) on Costa Rica territory . . . and on members of the Armed Forces of Costa Rica"; "gratuitous aggression" by Nicaragua; and "flagrant violations of the national territory" of Costa Rica. Numerous other examples of statements by Central American governments complaining of Nicaragua's aggression toward them, and additional evidence confirming those complaints, may be found in the U.S. Countermemorial and the annexes thereto.

Nicaragua has repeatedly made sanctimonious statements to this Court, including a sworn statement by Nicaragua's

---

Jurisdiction of the Court

Many countries have not accepted the jurisdiction of the Court, although reserving the right to accept it in a particular case. These countries include France, Italy, West Germany, Spain, Cuba, the Soviet Union, and the Soviet satellites. Countries that accepted the Court's jurisdiction, albeit with reservations, include Australia, India, Great Britain, and the United States.

C. Dickerman Williams, *National Review*, August 24, 1984

Foreign Minister, that Nicaragua is *not* engaged in armed attacks against its neighbors. As we have just shown, these statements are directly contradicted by the public statements of *all* of Nicaragua's neighbors and by *all* of the senior U.S. officials—in both the executive and legislative branches—with access to the full range of relevant diplomatic and intelligence information.

Contadora Negotiations

The bloodshed in Central America extends throughout Central America, and one of its principal causes is the aggression of Nicaragua. The question that all responsible statesmen must ask is, how can this bloodshed most effectively be ended? The states of Central America, including Nicaragua, have agreed that the multilateral Contadora negotiations offer the best hope for a lasting peace in the region. The UN Security Council, the Organization of American States, and, most recently, the Foreign Ministers of the European Community have all endorsed the Contadora negotations . . .

Nicaragua alone wishes to stop the Contadora negotiating process at the stage of an intermediate draft agreement. Under these circumstances, Nicaragua cannot plausibly contend that it is the United States that is blocking progress in the negotiations.

Just as it is Nicaragua alone that seeks to prevent further Contadora negotiations, it is Nicaragua alone that seeks to adjudicate bilateral aspects of those multilateral negotiations before this Court. Again, it is useful to quote the other Central American states in this regard. Thus, El Salvador stated in its letter to the Court of 17 September, 1984:

El Salvador is persuaded *in the considerations of its own survival as a nation* that to subject an isolated aspect of the Central American conflict to judicial determination at this time would cut straight across the best hopes for a peaceful solution . . . (Emphasis added.)

To the same effect, Honduras advised the Secretary General on 18 April 1984 as follows:

Once again the Government of Nicaragua is seeking to flout the Contadora negotiation process by attempting to bring the Central America crisis, essentially a political issue,

114

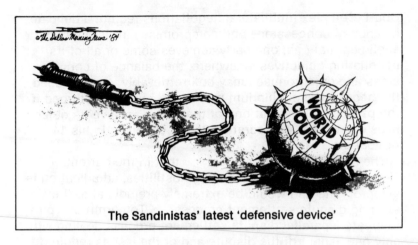

The Sandinistas' latest 'defensive device'

under the jurisdiction of the International Court of Justice. This is detrimental to the negotiations in progress and fails to recognize the resolutions of the United Nations and the Organization of American States or the full international endorsement that the Contadora peace process has so deservedly received.

In a press release of 16 April 1984 Guatemala stated:

The Central American issue should be discussed by the Contadora Group; (and) any attempt to seek another forum or international body in order to discuss security problems of a political, economic, and social nature has a negative impact on the Contadora process.

And Costa Rica advised the Court in April:

Whatever measures which the Court might adopt in the "case" presented for its consideration, taking such measures outside the context of the complete political and military situation that prevails in the Central American region, could become a distorting factor in the difficult equilibrium sought by the Forum of Contadora in a broader framework of solutions and could compromise, if not undertaken with prudence and equity, all possibilities of success for the "Forum of Contadora."

There is, therefore, *unanimous* agreement among the Central American states other than Nicaragua that adjudication of Nicaragua's claims by this Court seriously risks undermining the possibilities for Contadora's achievement of peace in Central America. Surely this apprehension will come as no surprise to the experienced statesmen and jurists of this

Court. Complex multilateral negotiations require a delicate balance of concessions and compromises. If, in the midst of such negotiations, one party achieves some or all of its negotiating objectives elsewhere, the balance of concessions and compromises may be irretrievably upset. Indeed, the negotiating equilibrium may be profoundly disturbed if the parties believe that one of them *may* achieve its objectives elsewhere. As Secretary Shultz observed in his 14 August affidavit:

The United States considers . . . that in the current circumstances involving ongoing hostilities, adjudication is inappropriate and would be extremely prejudicial to the existing dispute settlement process . . . To permit one party to create a parallel dispute settlement process dealing with only one aspect of the dispute and of the issues required to be addressed in a comprehensive solution would affect adversely the current multilateral and bilateral negotiating processes encompassed in the Contadora framework, and could, in the opinion of the United States, delay, if not forestall, an end to the fighting . . .

With the Court's permission, the United States would like to make one final prefatory remark. The United States has for many years been among the strongest supporters of this Court and of international adjudication generally . . .

Furthermore, it must be recalled that the judicial settlement of international disputes is but one of the proper means of peaceful settlement of certain international disputes. In certain circumstances, like those presented here, the UN Charter specifically requires other means, consistent with state practice of long duration. The various other means of peaceful settlement may, in many instances, be more likely to result in an effective, lasting resolution of a given dispute than the adversarial processes of bilateral adjudication. Among the other means of a peaceful settlement of international disputes endorsed by the Charter is negotiation, such as that now being conducted on a multilateral regionwide basis under the Contadora process. The United States wishes to emphasize that support of such a negotiating process, intended to resolve complex multilateral disputes on an agreed basis, is in no way inconsistent with the general support of the United States for international adjudication.

16

SANDINISTAS
AND U.S. POLICY

ECONOMIC SANCTIONS
ARE NEEDED

Langhorne A. Motley

*Langhorne A. Motley is the Assistant Secretary of State for
Inter-American Affairs. The following comments are excerp-
ted from testimony before the House Foreign Relations
Committee.*

Points to Consider

1. What specific economic sanctions were placed against
   Nicaragua?
2. How are the objectives of these sanctions described?
3. Why were the sanctions imposed?
4. What impact will they have on Nicaragua?

Excerpted from testimony by Langhorne A. Motley before the House
Foreign Affairs Committee, May 7, 1985.

The economic sanctions are an additional component of our continuing effort to induce the Nicaraguan government to change its policies and actions.

The economic sanctions affecting Nicaragua ordered by President Reagan on May 1 are part of our continuing diplomatic effort to use all appropriate political, economic and security measures to assist U.S. friends in Central America in defending themselves against the aggressive and destabilizing actions of the Sandinistas, Cubans and Soviets in Nicaragua.

The sanctions:

— prohibit imports into the U.S. of Nicaraguan goods and services and exports of goods from the U.S. to Nicaragua; and

— terminate air transportation to or from the U.S. by Nicaraguan air carriers and close our ports to all Nicaraguan flag vessels.

We have also notified the Government of Nicaragua of our intention to terminate our Treaty of Friendship, Commerce and Navigation.

These measures will remain in effect until we conclude that the government of Nicaragua has taken concrete steps that address our concerns and those of their neighbors.

I have attached to this prepared statement a copy of the President's Executive Order and of his report to the Congress pursuant to the International Emergency Economic Powers Act (IEEPA).

The President has assigned responsibility for the specific implementation of the actions under the IEEPA to the Secretary of the Treasury, who is represented at this hearing.

This prepared statement focuses on how these measures fit into U.S. policy and what their impact is likely to be.

"WELL, IT SEEMS SENATORS DODD AND TSONGAS AND A COUPLE OF OTHER CONGRESSMEN DON'T WANT ANOTHER 'VIETNAM' IN EL SALVADOR... THEY SAY THE SIGNS ARE RIGHT FOR NEGOTIATIONS."

The Sanctions as Part of U.S. Policy

The sanctions have three main objectives:

— To underscore to both friends and adversaries our determination to resist subversion and to protect our security and that of our friends;

— To reaffirm our opposition to Sandinista policies; and

— To maintain pressure on the Sandinistas as an inducement to change.

The basic policy of the United States is to support democracy, development and security in Central America. This policy has been developed over several years with bipartisan Congressional support and in close consultation with our neighbors in Central America. It is designed to help resolve that region's pervasive economic, social and political problems and to counter persistent Soviet and Cuban efforts to establish there totalitarian regimes and incorporate the region into the Soviet sphere of influence.

The sanctions against Nicaragua are the latest expression of this comprehensive U.S. policy. There has been no change in our basic policy toward Nicaragua. We do not seek to overthrow that country's government. We have no plans to impose any particular government in Managua. We do insist,

119

however, that the Government of Nicaragua change its behavior to:

— halt support for armed insurrection and subversion elsewhere in Central America;

— end its military ties with Cuba and the Soviet bloc and send home their military and security personnel;

— reverse its military build-up so as to restore the regional military balance; and

— respect democratic pluralism and observance of full political and human rights in Nicaragua.

Changes in these four areas are essential for peace in Central America and for constructive relations between our two nations. These are not goals we have set unilaterally. They are goals which have been consistently and unanimously repeated for several years now. In fact, the Central American countries, including the Nicaraguan government, agreed to all of them as objectives of the Contadora effort to resolve the conflicts in the region.

We have repeatedly urged the *comandantes,* in public and in private bilateral contacts, to respect their 1979 promises to the Nicaraguan people and to the OAS — commitments they reaffirmed in signing the 1983 Contadora Document of Objectives. To date the Sandinistas have rejected our appeals and those of their neighbors with the same intrasigence they have shown toward their fellow Nicaraguans — including their country's Roman Catholic bishops.

The economic sanctions are an additional component of our continuing effort to induce the Nicaraguan government to change its policies and actions. And changes in Sandinista behavior are essential for the peace process in Central America to succeed.

The Nicaraguan Threat

Nicaragua's efforts to subvert its neighbors, its destabilizing military buildup, its close military ties to the Soviet bloc, and its totalitarian behavior represent a clear threat to the security of Central America and therefore to the United States. Over a period of almost six years, the policies and actions of the Nicaraguan government have not moderated,

Largest Trading Partner

While U.S. trade with Nicaragua has been declining in recent years the U.S. nevertheless is Nicaragua's largest trading partner, accounting for 14 percent of Nicaragua's global trade, totalling $168 million. . .

The sanctions, therefore, are a meaningful economic pressure point because they alter trading relationships that have, in many cases, been in place for decades and, thereby, force Nicaragua to restructure part of its already faltering economy.

Joseph F. Dennin , U.S. Department of Commerce, May 7, 1985

but have become increasingly intense, heightening the threat to U.S. national security and foreign policy interests.

President Ortega's visit to Moscow, on the heels of a debate in the United States Congress over concerns in this country about the directions in which Nicaragua is moving and the most appropriate U.S. response, confirms both the Sandinistas' determination to continue their aggression in concert with the Soviet bloc, and their belief that the United States lacks the resolve to defend U.S. interests and the interests of U.S. allies in Central America.

This past month has furnished numerous fresh indications of this disturbing pattern:

— In mid-April, seven agents of the Nicaraguan state security service were captured in Honduras. The Nicaraguan agents admitted that this was the third secret trip in six months in which they had transported arms from Nicaragua to Honduran guerillas, whom they also assisted in recruiting and training;

— The Sandinista *comandantes* reaffirmed their rejection of any Church-mediated dialogue with the Nicaraguan opposition;

— The Soviet Union delivered to Nicaragua additional MI-8/17 military helicopters, while

— East Germany delivered a large shipment of military transport equipment; and finally

— On April 29, during Daniel Ortega's visit to Moscow, TASS announced new ties between Nicaragua and the Soviet Union.

These events, like the Sandinistas' rejection of the President's peace initiative, must be considered along with the pressure that Nicaragua's military buildup places on the democratic nations of the region. They are continuing manifestations of the urgent threat that Nicaragua poses to the security of the region, and, therefore, to the security and foreign policy of the United States.

This pattern of threatening behavior is not the sort of normal, ongoing difficulty we sometimes experience with other nations which do not share our views. Rather, it constitutes an emergency situation which is incompatible with normal commercial ties between our two countries.

As secretary Shultz said on April 25, perception of American weakness is "the most destabilizing factor on the global scene."

The *comandantes* must understand that the United States has both the means and the resolve to protect its interests in Central America.

SANDINISTAS AND U.S. POLICY

ECONOMIC SANCTIONS VIOLATE NICARAGUA'S RIGHTS

Sandinista Leadership

The following comments were taken from a statement by the revolutionary government of Nicaragua and the national leadership of the Sandinista National Liberation Front (Frente Sandinista de Liberacion Nacional, FSLN).

Points to Consider

1. Why is the U.S. imposing an economic blockade?
2. What effect will the blockade have on Nicaragua?
3. How should nations of Latin America react to the blockade?

FSLN, "Economic Blockade," *Granma,* May 12, 1985.

The boycott ordered by President Reagan against our small but dignified nation is a premeditated step that puts the U.S. government on the road to direct military intervention in Nicaragua.

The president of the United States, resorting in an absurd and disproportionate manner to the emergency powers granted by federal laws to deal with threats to national security and the internal stability of his immense and powerful country, has officially informed Nicaragua of his decision to impose a new series of economic reprisals which include a total suspension of trade and air and maritime traffic between the two countries.

In addition to the fact that this measure is an abuse of the United States' own laws and was adopted in defiance of the norms and conventions which govern international law and economic order, the boycott ordered by President Reagan against our small but dignified nation is a premeditated step that puts the U.S. government on the road to direct military intervention in Nicaragua.

That is the only conclusion which can be drawn from the official notice dated May 1, 1985 which the State Department sent to the Nicaraguan Foreign Ministry, stating that if Nicaragua does not concretely fulfill the conditions stipulated in the note, the likelihood for a peaceful settlement in Central America will fade. This means that if Nicaragua does not yield to the will of the United States, President Reagan assumes the right to military intervention in Nicaragua and to declare total war on us . . .

U. S. Conditions

The conditions which the president of the United States wants to impose on Nicaragua for the lifting of the sanctions which are contained in the May 1 note are the same arrogant and arbitrary impositions as always aimed at trampling upon our rights as a sovereign country by use of force and coercion, the attempt to dictate norms conceived by the U.S.

124

government itself to control Nicaragua's domestic political order, manage our international relations as it sees fit and draw up a list for us of who our friends and enemies should be.

With the strength derived from justice and right, in our status as a moral power — because what we lack in material wealth and military resources is compensated for by the resolute dignity of an entire people — as of now we say as we have always said, that we will never tolerate foreign interference or accept a cowardly peace.

The measures of economic aggression ordered by President Reagan and the others he is planning in the near future will certainly lead to more suffering, shortages and limitations for our country; for our efforts to transform society; for the development of a new economy which we want to base on the multiple participation of all Nicaraguans and which we continue to view as a mixed economy; for the promotion of agrarian reform, agricultural production, the functioning of industry, forestry, mining and fishing, the extension of health and education services; and for our efforts to secure enough

goods for all. There will be difficulties and problems of a new dimension which will be added to those which have been building up in the social and economic life of the country since President Reagan began his mercenary war against Nicaragua upon taking office in the United States, a war which has already led to so much destruction, desolation, death and so many orphans.

This new escalation in economic aggression is now viciously directed against Nicarguans of all social sectors, of all classes, of all productive forces, against the workers in the city and the countryside, small and middle-level farmers, cooperatives, businessmen and professional associations. It is a blow against Nicaraguan society, against the nation. It is a blind reprisal against Nicaragua and all its citizens in an effort to destroy our efforts, dreams and hopes . . .

We will find new markets for our export products as we have been doing, diversifying foreign trade; we will rationalize our imports and in a responsible and creative manner replace what we can't import; we will be more zealous than ever in the adminsitration of our limited resources; and the Sandinista Front, its leaders, activists and members and the officials of the revolutionary government will set the finest examples of constant devotion to work and austerity. It will be our forces, the energy of the people which will give us the answers and the solutions. This is a task for everyone, all worthy Nicaraguans, the whole nation.

Those who exclude themselves from this patriotic call, those who in this hour of trial are more responsive to the voice of the aggressor than to the call of their own attacked homeland, are abandoning their post, their place in the ranks of national dignity . . .

Financial Power

The financial power of the United States is also being used to oppress the countries of Latin America. The unjust and immoral foreign debt, which already constitutes an unbearable weight on the shoulders of our peoples, is being used as a threatening weapon of blackmail and is becoming a strategic element in the great imperial plot to destroy Latin American independence.

We realize we represent an example. We are not the strongest link in the continental chain, but precisely because we are carrying forward a national revolution in a weak small country on this continent, we are in fact a vital link and must therefore multiply our forces and never yield, because that would mean yielding the historic possibility of Latin American independence that is now being tested in Nicaragua at a cost of so much blood.

We call on the nations and peoples of Latin America not to leave Nicaragua in the solitude desired by the U.S. government so it can strike at us with impunity. In order to prepare this attack it has militarily occupied Honduras and increased its naval and ground forces in the Central American region, building airports, weapons warehouses and fuel deposits, storing tanks, armored cars, helicopters and planes.

We call on the U.S. Congress and people to do honor to the democratic principles of their country, by stopping in every way possible the war escalation being implemented by President Reagan against Nicaragua. They must not permit the abusive use of U.S. laws to attack a country such as ours which only wants to live and transform itself in peace and which does not desire hatred or war with any country.

Plan to Invade Nicaragua

A former CIA analyst said Monday that an agency plan to invade Nicaragua and destabilize its Sandinista government was put into effect under the guise of preventing Nicaraguan arms shipments to Salvadoran guerrillas.

He also said there was "no credible evidence" that the Nicaraguan government had provided significant quantities of arms to those guerrillas for at least the last four years.

David Macmichael, who worked for the Central Intelligence Agency from 1981 to 1983, had testified Friday at the World Court that the plan to send 1,500 armed troops into Nicaragua had the approval of President Reagan. He did not specify the intended makeup of the force.

Chicago Tribune, September 17, 1985

SANDINISTAS
AND U.S. POLICY

SAVING FREEDOM
IN NICARAGUA

Ronald Reagan

The following comments were made by President Reagan before the International Longshoremen's Association (ILA) in Hollywood, Florida.

Points to Consider

1. What are conditions like in Central America?
2. What promises were made by the Sandinistas?
3. What is the link between Nicaragua and El Salvador?
4. How can freedom be saved in Nicaragua?

From a speech by President Reagan, July 18, 1983.

People throughout Latin America are waiting to see if Republicans and Democrats in this country can work together to make the United States what it should be: a loyal friend and reliable defender of democracy and human decency.

Our democracy encompasses many freedoms—freedom of speech, of religion, of assembly, and of so many other liberties that we often take for granted. These are rights that should be shared by all mankind. This union has always patriotically stood up for those freedoms. And that's why I want to talk to you today about freedom not in the United States, but in a part of the world that's very close and very important to us—Central America.

We all know that Central America suffers from decades of poverty, social deprivation, and political instability. And because these problems weren't dealt with positively, they are now being exploited by the enemies of freedom. We cannot afford the luxury of turning away from our neighbors' struggles as if they didn't matter. If we do turn away, we'll pay a terrible price for our neglect . . .

There is still time for the people of Latin America to build a prosperous, peaceful, and free future. And we have an obligation to help them—for our own sake as well as theirs.

People throughout Latin America are waiting to see if Republicans and Democrats in this country can work together to make the United States what it should be: a loyal friend and reliable defender of democracy and human decency. I believe that we must exercise that leadership. And the time is now.

Sandinista Revolution

Since I spoke to the Congress in April, Cuba has sent one of its best known combat generals to Nicaragua. More Cuban soldiers and Soviet suppliers have arrived in Nicaragua. This cannot be allowed to continued.

Tomorrow, July 19th, is the fourth anniversary of the Sandinista revolution. This was a revolution that promised to bring freedom to the Nicaraguan people; history will call it the revolution of broken promises. Tomorrow the nine military commanders who rule Nicaragua with Cuban and Soviet power will indulge in boastful revolutionary rhetoric. But there are few left who will believe them. The consensus throughout the hemisphere is that while the Sandinistas promised their people freedom, all they've done is replace the former dictatorship with their own—a dictatorship of counterfeit revolutionaries who wear fatigues, and drive around in Mercedes sedans and Soviet tanks, and whose cur-

Source: U.S. Department of State

rent promise is to spread their brand of "revolution" throughout Central America.

What kind of freedom have the Sandinistas established? Just ask the 1,300 stevedores at the Nicaraguan port of Corinto. Last month, their union assembly was packed with Sandinistas and six union leaders were arrested. Their presumed crime was trying to develop ties with independent trade unions, including some here affiliated with the AFL-CIO. I can tell you one thing. If all the longshoremen in Corinto are like Teddy Gleason [ILA president], the Sandinistas have got a real fight on their hands. Matter of fact, if they've got one like you Teddy, they may be like those two fellows who were up sawing on a limb, and one of them fell off. And there was a wildcat down below, and there were sounds of struggle coming up, and the one still up on the limb called down and said, "Hold on." And he said, "Hold on?" He said, "Come down and tell me how to let him go."

What kind of democracy is it? Ask the Nicaraguan refugees who've risked starvation and attack to escape to Honduras. Let me read to you directly from a newspaper article: ". . . one Nicaraguan man—still filthy, ragged, and, above all, hungry after an odyssey that began 5 weeks ago—breathed a note of thanks: 'God has smiled on us.' " Imagine, with barely clothes on his back and nothing in his stomach, he believed God had smiled on him because he had arrived in free, democratic Honduras.

This man fled Nicaragua in May with many others when they learned the Sandinistas planned to relocate their villages. Let me quote again what one of the refugees had to say: "We left everything. We left the pigs, the corn, the animals . . . This year they wouldn't let us plant, because they wanted us to move closer to the military bases, they wanted us to be in the militia, and we did not want to be executioners."

When the Sandinistas first took power, all their neighbors hoped that they would embrace democracy as they promised. In the first year and a half after the revolution, the United States sent $118 million worth of emergency relief and recovery aid to Nicaragua, more than provided by any other country in the world. But the Sandinistas had lied. They rejected their pledges to their own people, to the Organization of American States (OAS), and to the world.

The Promises

Let me say a few more words about those specific promises. The Sandinistas had promised the Organization of American States that they would hold elections and grant all human rights that go with a democracy. In short, they literally made a contract to establish a true democracy. The dictator Somoza was then persuaded by the OAS to resign, and the government was turned over to the revolutionaries and recognized officially by the OAS.

So far so good. But then, one faction of the revolutionaries—backed by Cuba and the Soviet Union—seized total power and ousted their revolutionary comrades who'd been fighting to establish a real democracy. Nicaragua is today a nation abusing its own people and its neighbors. The guerrilla bands fighting in Nicaragua are trying to restore the true revolution and keep the promises made to OAS. Isn't it time that all of us in the Americas worked together to hold Nicaragua accountable for the promises made and broken 4 years ago?

The Link Between Nicaragua and El Salvador

There is a vital link between what's happening in Nicaragua and what's happening in El Salvador. And the link is very simple: The dictators of Nicaragua are actively trying to destroy the budding democracy in neighboring El Salvador. El Salvador is moving toward a more open society and government in the midst of a foreign-supported guerrilla war. National presidential elections are planned. Through their peace commissions, they've offered to talk even to the violent opposition about participation in the forthcoming elections. They have implemented an effective land reform program which has provided land for over half a million Salvadorans, and they've given amnesty to former guerrillas.

This is El Salvador's revolution—it is one that is building democracy. Contrast this with the corrupted revolution in Nicaragua—one which has repressed human liberties, denied free unions and free elections, censored the press, threatened its neighbors, and violated public pledges.

SANDINISTAS AND U.S. POLICY

IMPERIALISM IN NICARAGUA

The People

The following statement deals with the history of U.S. military interventions in Nicaragua. It appeared in The People, *a publication of the Socialist Labor Party.*

Points to Consider

1. When and why did the U.S. send military forces to Nicaragua?
2. Who was Augusto Cesar Sandino?
3. When and why did U.S. marines leave Nicaragua?
4. Who was Anastasio Somoza?

"Nicaragua: Where Are We Heading?" *The People,* February 16, 1985.

133

*U.S. military forces were finally withdrawn
in 1925 only to return in 1926 once again to
install a government totally dependent
upon this country.*

Feb. 21 marks the anniversary of the murder of the
Nicaraguan patriot Augusto Cesar Sandino on Feb. 21, 1934,
by agents of the dictator Anastasio Somoza.

Americans ought to reflect upon that occurrence and the
events that preceded it because they contain important
lessons for us all. One can never understand what is going
on in Nicaragua today or why the U.S. government is
threatening this small nation now unless one understands
some of its history. It is not history of which Americans can
be proud, but it is history nonetheless.

During the 19th century, long before it became a world
power, the United States established important commercial
interests in Central America. In 1855 an American adven-
turer, William Walker, aided by American business interests,
invaded Nicaragua with a private army and for a brief period
set himself up as its dictator.

Throughout the late 19th century Nicaragua repeatedly
experienced periods of internal turmoil. At the same time,
the power of U.S. business interests grew to the point where
they eventually controlled the Nicaraguan economy. In 1912,
during one of Nicaragua's many civil wars, the United States
sent Marines into Nicaragua on the double pretext that it
had been requested to do so by Nicaragua's president and
that the U.S. forces were there to protect American lives and
property (much as the United States did in Grenada in
October 1983). The 1912 invasion turned into a 13-year
occupation during which the United States installed a pup-
pet government in Nicaragua that virtually sold the country
to American business interests.

U.S. military forces were finally withdrawn in 1925 only to
return in 1926 once again to install a government totally
dependent upon this country.

134

Sandino

It is at this point that Sandino stepped upon the stage of history. He was no military man or politician. He was a simple man with peasant roots that ran deeply into the soil of Nicaragua. He was a patriot who loved his country. He had been a farmer and cowhand and had also worked as a miner, watchman and oil well rigger.

At the time, Sandino was 32 years old and virtually unknown in Nicaragua. He joined the growing resistance to the U.S. occupation and when that resistance was ready to sell out to the United States, Sandino and a small group of nationalists established an independent guerrilla army that continued to resist the U.S. occupation. From 1928 until 1933 Sandino's "army" fought both U.S. forces and their Nicaraguan puppets. The American forces were withdrawn in 1933. They left behind what was to become the notorious National Guard, set up and trained by U.S. Marines and commanded by Anastasio Somoza, hand picked by the American ambassador to Nicaragua.

Sandino made the tragic mistake of believing that the end of U.S. occupation also brought an end to the suffering of

A Guerrilla War

In 1927 a guerrilla war was unleashed in the jungles and mountains of Nicaragua by a ragged and hungry group of compatriots who grew in number from 26 to 3,000—against 6,000 well-fed, well-trained, and well-equipped U.S. Marines. For seven years the invaders were held at bay. The leader of this remarkable guerrilla band was Augusto Cesar Sandino. A mechanic and miner of peasant and Indian stock, he never lost sight of his prime objective: to rid Nicaragua of the U.S. army of occupation and the business interests it was protecting.

Gregorio Selser, Sandino, *Monthly Review Press,* 1981

Map of Nicaragua shows provinces and Ocotal, scene of most recent CIA-led attack. Sandinistas consider provinces of Nueva Segovia, Madriz, Matagalpa, Jinotega, Chontales, Rio San Juan, and southern Zelaya to be "zones of permanent conflict."

Source: The Militant

Nicaragua. He and his followers laid down their arms and joined in a cooperative farming project. On the night of Feb. 21, 1934, he was murdered by Somoza's troops as he left a conference at the National Palace in Managua to which he had been invited. His murder was planned and executed by Somoza with the full knowledge and support of the U.S. ambassador and his government.

By 1936 Anastasio Somoza was entrenched as dictator of Nicaragua. He and his two sons continued to rule until their infamous regime was overthrown in July 1979. The movement that destroyed the Somoza dictatorship and that now governs Nicaragua — the Sandinista National Liberation Front — took its name and inspiration from Sandino. And it is this government that the United States now seeks to destroy for the same reasons that it could not tolerate Sandino — namely, his opposition to U.S. dominance and exploitation.

The American media during the 1920s and 1930s denounced Sandino as a "bandit" much like the media today denounce as a "terrorist" anyone who opposes U.S. policy. The U.S. government at that time spread the lie that the trouble in Nicaragua was fomented by "radical" Mexico much the way the present administration blames Cuba for U.S. difficulties in Nicaragua.

Nicaragua's National Hero

February 21 marks the 50th anniversary of the murder of Augusto Cesar Sandino, national hero of Nicaragua. Sandino organized an army in 1927 to drive out the U.S. Marines, who had occupied Nicaragua in 1926. While the wealthy Nicaragua ruling families were afraid to struggle for national sovereignty, Sandino organized workers and peasants in battles to oust the marines, who finally withdrew in 1933, after setting up the notorious National Guard headed by the Somoza family. On Feb. 21, 1934, Sandino was assassinated by the guard.

The Militant, March 2, 1984

Oppose Intervention

Don't be fooled by the rantings of the Reagan administration that seeks to destroy Nicaraguan independence by its support for direct military action or, for that matter, by the glib talk of Democratic liberals who seek to strangle that independence by naval and economic blockades. Examine closely the reasons why the United States behaves as it does in the Third World and how that behavior is linked directly to the very nature of our economic system.

Yes, American people must oppose U.S. intervention in Nicaragua; but we must also learn the lessons of history or we're going to be forced to relive old mistakes. Don't allow this "antiwar movement" to disappear, as did the anti-Vietnam War movement of the 1960s and 1970s, without ever getting to the heart of the problem.

INTERPRETING EDITORIAL CARTOONS

This activity may be used as an individualized study guide for students in libraries and resource centers or as a discussion catalyst in small group and classroom discussions.

Although cartoons are usually humorous, the main intent of most political cartoonists is not to entertain. Cartoons express serious social comment about important issues. Using graphic and visual arts, the cartoonist expresses opinions and attitudes. By employing an entertaining and often light-hearted visual format, cartoonists may have as much or more impact on national and world issues as editorial and syndicated columnists.

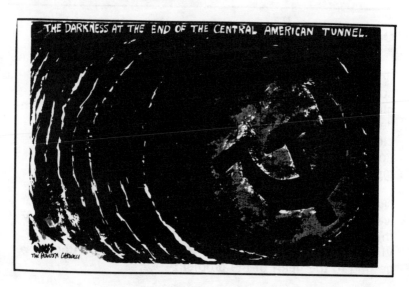

Points to Consider

1. Examine the two cartoons in this activity.

2. How would you describe the message of each cartoon? Try to describe each message in one to three sentences.

3. Do you agree with the message expressed in either cartoon? Why or why not?

4. Do either of the cartoons support the author's point of view in any of the readings in this publication? If the answer is yes, be specific about which reading or readings and why.

5. Are any of the readings in chapter four in basic agreement with either of the cartoons?

Barricada/Róger

139

CHAPTER 5

NICARAGUA: A THREAT TO OUR SECURITY?

20 NICARAGUA: A THREAT TO OUR SECURITY?

AIDING THE REBELS WILL NOT WORK

Edgar Chamorro

Edgar Chamorro was raised in Nicaragua. At age nineteen he joined the Jesuit order and later became a priest. He was unhappy with the Sandinistas and claims that the CIA persuaded him to take a leadership position in the Nicaraguan Democratic Force, FDN. Rebel groups fighting against the Sandinistas are often referred to as contras. The following comments are excerpted from Edgar Chamorro's written statement to the World Court in the case Nicaragua v. the United States of America.

Points to Consider

1. How did the Nicaraguan Democratic Force (FDN) get recruits?
2. What role did the CIA play in the FDN activities?
3. What military activities did the CIA carry out against Nicaragua?
4. Why did Edgar Chamorro become disillusioned with the FDN?
5. Why will U.S. support for the rebels fail to accomplish their objectives?

Excerpted from an affidavit of Edgar Chamorro before the International Court of Justice, September 5, 1985.

The FDN turned out to be an instrument of the United States Government and, specifically, of the CIA. It was created by the CIA, it was supplied, equipped, armed and trained by the CIA and its activities —both political and military—were directed and controlled by the CIA.

1982 was a year of transition for the FDN. From a collection of small, disorganized and ineffectual bands of ex-National Guardsmen, the FDN grew into a well-organized, well-armed, well-equipped and well-trained fighting force of approximately 4,000 men capable of inflicting great harm on Nicaragua. This was due entirely to the CIA, which organized, armed, equipped, trained and supplied us. After the initial recruitment of ex-Guardsmen from throughout the region (to serve as officers or commanders of military units), efforts were made to recruit "foot soldiers" for the force from inside Nicaragua. Some Nicaraguans joined the force voluntarily, either because of dissatisfaction with the Nicaraguan Government, family ties with leaders of the force, promises of food, clothing, boots and weapons, or a combination of these reasons. Many other members of the force were recruited forcibly. FDN units would arrive at an undefended village, assemble all the residents in the town square and then proceed to kill—in full view of the others —all persons suspected of working for the Nicaraguan Government or the FSLN, including police, local militia members, party members, health workers, teachers, and farmers from government-sponsored cooperatives. In this atmosphere, it was not difficult to persuade those able-bodied men left alive to return with the FDN units to their base camps in Honduras and enlist in the force. This was, unfortunately, a widespread practice that accounted for many recruits. The FDN received all of its weapons from the CIA.

The CIA was directly involved in our military tactics. The agency repeatedly ordered us to move our troops inside Nicaragua and to keep them there as long as possible. After

142

our offensive at the end of 1982 was turned back, almost all of our troops were in Honduras and our own officers believed that they needed more training and more time before they would be ready to return to Nicaragua. The FDN officers were overruled by the CIA, however. The agency told us that we had to move our men back into Nicaragua and keep fighting. We had no choice but to obey. In 1983, the CIA instructed us not to destroy farms or crops because that would be politically counterproductive. In 1984, however, we were instructed to destroy export crops (especially coffee and tobacco), and to attack farms and cooperatives. Accordingly, we changed our tactics in 1984.

Paramilitary Activities

In July 1983, we were visited in Tegucigalpa by Duane Clarridge, the CIA official, based in Washington, who was in charge of the agency's military and paramilitary activities against Nicaragua.

He said the Agency was considering a plan "to sink ships" bringing oil to Nicaragua, but that one problem with this plan was that if a ship belonging to the Soviet Union were sunk it could trigger a serious international incident. Clarridge said that the CIA was also considering an attack on Nicaragua's sole oil refinery, located near Managua. . .

In September 1983, the CIA blew up the pipeline at Puerto Sandino, just as Clarridge had advised us it would. The actual opertives were Agency employees of Hispanic descent, referred to within the Agency as "Unilaterally Controlled Latino Assets" or UCLAs. These UCLAs, specially trained underwater demolitions experts, were dispatched from a CIA "mother ship" that took them to within striking distance of their target. Although the FDN had nothing whatsoever to do with this operation, we were instructed by the CIA to publicly claim responsibility in order to cover the CIA's involvement. We did. In October, C.I.A. UCLAs attacked Nicaragua's oil storage tanks at Corinto, also on the Pacific Coast. This was a combined sea and air attack involving the use of rockets. It was a complete success; all of the tanks were destroyed and enormous quantities of oil were consumed by fire. Again, the CIA instructed us to publicly claim responsibility, and we did. Later in October, there was another UCLA attack on Puerto Sandino, which again resulted in the demolition of the oil pipeline. We again claimed responsibility per instructions from the CIA. Subsequently, the UCLAs attacked Nicaraguan Government military facilities at Potosi and radio antennas at Las Casitas. We again were told to claim responsibility and we did. . .

On January 5, 1984, at 2:00 a.m., the CIA deputy station chief of Tegucigalpa, the agent I knew as "George," woke me up at my house in Tegucigalpa and handed me a press release in excellent Spanish. I was surprised to read that we —the FDN—were taking credit for having mined several Nicaraguan harbors. "George" told me to rush to our clandestine radio station and read this announcement before the Sandinistas broke the news. The truth is that we played no role in the mining of the harbors. But we did as instructed and broadcast the communique about the mining of the harbors. Ironically, approximately two months later,

---

Contra Aid Prolongs War

The best course for the United States is to distance itself from the conflict, encourage political diaglogue and support Latin American countries in their effort to prevent a regional war.

My experience as a former rebel leader convinced me that the Nicaraguan Democratic Force cannot contribute to the democratization of Nicaragua. The rebels are in the hands of former national guardsmen who control the contra army, stifle internal dissent and intimidate or murder those who dare oppose them. The rebels have been subject to manipulation by the CIA . . .

The funds voted by Congress are simply another vehicle to prolong this war. The only assistance worthy of the name "humanitarian aid" is help for victims on both sides.

Edgar Chamorro, *Mineapolis Star & Tribune,* July 9, 1985

---

after a Soviet ship struck one of the mines, the same agent instructed us to deny that one of "our" mines had damaged the ship to avoid an international incident.

Military Assistance

In May 1984 the United States Congress voted not to provide more assistance to the CIA for military and paramilitary activities against Nicaragua. Many of us became worried about receiving continued support from the United States Government and we expressed these concerns to our CIA colleagues in Tegucigalpa. We were repeatedly assured by the station chief and his deputies, in the strongest possible terms, that we would not be abandoned and that the United States Government would find a way to continue its support. At around this time we were visited by Ronald F. Lehman II, a Special Assistant to the President of the United States who was serving then on the National Security Council. Mr. Lehman assured us that President Reagan remained committed to removing the Sandinistas from power. He told us that President Reagan was unable at that time to publicly express the full extent of his commitment to us because of the upcoming presidential elections in the United States. But, Mr. Lehman told us, as soon as the elections were over, President Reagan would publicly endorse our effort to remove the Sandinistas from power and see to it that we received all the support that was necessary for that purpose. . .

FDN Atrocities

A major part of my job as communications officer was to work to improve the image of the FDN forces. This was challenging, because it was standard FDN practice to kill prisoners and suspected Sandinista collaborators. In talking with officers in the FDN camps along the Honduran border, I frequently heard offhand remarks like, "Oh, I cut his throat." The CIA did not discourage such tactics. To the contrary, the Agency severely criticized me when I admitted to the press that the FDN had regularly kidnapped and executed agrarian reform workers and civilians. We were told that the only way to defeat the Sandinistas was to use the tactics the Agency attributed to "Communist" insurgencies elsewhere: kill, kidnap, rob and torture.

These tactics were reflected in an operations manual prepared for our forces by a CIA agent who used the name "John Kirkpatrick." I assisted "Kirkpatrick" in translating certain parts of the manual, and the manuscript was typed by my secretary. The manual was entitled: "Psychological Operations in Guerrilla Warfare." It advocated "explicit and implicit terror" against the civilian population, including assassination of government employees and sympathizers. Before the manual was distributed, I attempted to excise two passages that I thought were immoral and dangerous, at pages 70 and 71. One recommended hiring professional criminals. The other advocated killing some of our own colleagues to create martyrs for the cause. I did not particularly want to be "martyred" by the CIA. So I locked up all the copies of the manual and hired two youths to cut out the offending pages and glue in expurgated pages. About 2,000 copies of the manual, with only those two passages changed, were then distributed to FDN troops. Upon reflec-

By Bill Sanders, © by and permission of News America Syndicate

tion, I found many of the tactics advocated in the manual to be offensive, and I complained to the CIA station chief in Tegucigalpa. The station chief defended "Kirkpatrick" and the manual, and no action was ever taken in response to my complaints. In fact, the practices advocated in the manual were employed by FDN troops. Many civilians were killed in cold blood. Many others were tortured, mutilated, raped, robbed or otherwise abused.

As time went on, I became more and more troubled by the frequent reports I received of atrocities committed by our troops against civilians and against Sandinista prisoners. Calero and Bermudez refused to discuss the subject with me, so I went straight to our unit commanders as they returned from combat missions inside Nicaragua and asked them about their activities. I was saddened by what I was told. The atrocities I had heard about were not isolated incidents, but reflected a consistent pattern of behavior by our troops. There were unit commanders who openly bragged about their murders, mutilations, etc. When I questioned them about the propriety or wisdom of doing those things they told me it was the only way to win this war, that the best way to win the loyalty of the civilian population was to intimidate it and make it fearful of us. I complained to Calero and Bermudez, and to the CIA station chief about these activities, but nothing was done to stop them. In June 1984, Clarridge visited us again. Although he was well aware of the terrorist tactics the FDN troops were employing, he spoke warmly to Bermudez: "Well done, Colonel," I remember him saying, "Keep it up. Your boys are doing fine." It was the last time I saw him. . .

CIA Control

When I agreed to join the FDN in 1981, I had hoped that it would be an organization of Nicaraguans, controlled by Nicaraguans, and dedicated to our own objectives which we ourselves would determine. I joined on the understanding that the United States Government would supply us the means necessary to defeat the Sandinistas and replace them as a government, but I believed that we would be our own masters. I turned out to be mistaken. The FDN turned out to be an instrument of the United States Government and, specifically, of the CIA. It was created by the CIA, it was supplied, equipped, armed and trained by the CIA and its activities—both political and military—were directed and controlled by the CIA. Those Nicaraguans who were chosen (by the CIA) for leadership positions within the organization —namely, Calero and Bermudez—were those who best demonstrated their willingness to unquestioningly follow the instructions of the CIA. They, like the organization itself, became nothing more than executioners of the CIA's orders. The organization became so thoroughly dependent on the United States Government and its continued support that, if that support were terminated, the organization would not only be incapable of conducting any military or paramilitary activities against Nicaragua, but it would immediately begin to disintegrate. It could not exist without the support and direction of the United States Government.

I became more and more distanced from the FDN in the second half of 1984. I had, for all intents and purposes, ceased to be a part of the organization. Finally, on November 20, 1984, I received a letter stating that the political directorate had decided to relieve me of my duties. I made no protest.

My opposition to the Nicaraguan Government continues. I oppose its policies and programs and I would like to see it removed or replaced. This should be accomplished, however, by the Nicaraguan people themselves, and not by the United States Government or by its instruments, including the FDN, which follow its dictates and serve its interests instead of those of the Nicaraguan people. My presentation of this testimony to the International Court of Justice is not an expression of support or sympathy for the present Nicaraguan Government or its case against the United States. It is a result of my commitment to tell the truth, to all interested parties, about my personal experiences in the FDN.

Whatever the best solution for the Nicaraguan people may be, I am convinced that it can only come about on the basis of truth, and that those of us with relevant personal experience are under a moral obligation to make the truth known.

NICARAGUA: A THREAT TO OUR SECURITY?

THE CASE FOR CONTRA SUPPORT

Joshua Muravchik

Joshua Muravchik is the author of a forthcoming book about U.S. human rights policies. He argues for military and economic support for the contras.

Points to Consider

1. What was the containment policy?
2. How did the policy of "detente" differ from containment?
3. What alternative policy toward communism does the author suggest?
4. Why should the U.S. give assistance to the contras?

The Sandinistas have not yet turned Nicaragua into a totalitarian state, but there is little doubt that this is their goal.

By shedding the pretense that U.S. aid to the Nicaraguan rebels could aim at any goal other than the overthrow of the Sandinista government, President Reagan has strengthened the case for aid.

He has also helped us focus on the heart of the matter. Should the United States encourage the overthrow of Communist governments where we can? To me, both the history of our relations with the Soviet Union and the particular circumstances in Central America argue strongly that we should.

Both Sides

Both sides of the debate have been clarified in recent weeks. House majority leader Jim Wright took issue with the president: "I don't think we have any call to appoint ourselves as God's avenging angels and reform by force any government with whom we disagree." Secretary of State George Shultz spoke for the other side, noting that such opposition to aiding the "contras" is in effect to accept the "Brezhnev doctrine." It is, as Shultz aptly put it, to accept the Kremlin's notion that "What's mine is mine. What's yours is up for grabs."

The implications of this doctrine have grown more ominous since the American policy of containment expired on the battlefields of Vietnam. In adopting the containment policy, the United States decided to avoid challenging the integrity of the Soviet empire — which then lay entirely under the shadow or the feet of the Red Army — but to resist its expansion. As George Kennan, who first formulated the policy, put it, we would "confront the Russians with unalterable counterforce at every point where they show signs of encroaching upon the interests of a peaceful and stable world."

The hope, said Kennan, was to "increase enormously the strains under which Soviet policy must operate" and thereby "promote tendencies which must eventually find their outlet in either the breakup or the gradual mellowing of Soviet power."

The Soviet System

Some significant "mellowing" of the Soviet domestic system did indeed occur after Stalin's death, but the Soviet Union's relentless drive to expand its empire and to abet the seizure of power by Communists wherever possible has outlived the policy of containment.

As a result, in the mid-1970s the United States turned away from containment and toward detente, hoping, as then Secretary of State Henry Kissinger put it, "to create a vested interest in mutual restraint." But even had it prospered, detente offered little hope for solving the problem that containment aimed to solve: Soviet officials stated repeatedly that detente did not obligate them to cease supporting efforts by Communists to seize power where they did not already hold it.

Source: U.S. Department of State

President Jimmy Carter tried his own version of detente, more conciliatory than the Kissinger version, but its futility — its uselessness in inhibiting Soviet expansion — became apparent even to Carter with the invasion of Afghanistan.

Since then, U.S. policy has grown more assertive and our arsenals are being restocked. But there is no prospect of a return to containment. Even had we the will, the balance of power makes it impossible for us to parry the Russians at every point of their choosing.

Have we, then, no alternative but to resign ourselves to a gradual and inexorable increase in the number of Communist countries — an increase that could eventually shift the balance of power decisively against the United States? This might take a long time, but even in the short run there may be devastating consequences. How can we accept asymmetrical rules that allow countries to go from being non-Communist to Communist, but never the other direction?

Such asymmetry works to sap the morale of non-Communist forces and to validate communism's claim to be the wave of the future.

The Alternative

There is an alternative. The network of Communist governments in the Soviet camp now extends far beyond the shadow of the Red Army, into Africa and Central America. This network can be attacked at its fringes, if there are indigenous forces willing to do so, without the risk of provoking a military confrontation between the United States and the Soviet Union. This offers the basis for a strategy that, in the absence of containment, might still prevent the relentless accretion of Soviet power. And the successful overthrow of communism by indigenous forces in even one country might do incalculable damage to communism's historicist mystique.

Nicaragua

This argues strongly that giving the Nicaraguan rebels as much support as they need is very much in the interest of the United States. But that is not the only reason to aid the contras. The well-being of the Nicaraguan people is also very much at issue here.

The Sandinistas have not yet turned Nicaragua into a totalitarian state, but there is little doubt that this is their goal. The repressive manipulation of food rationing, the creation of a vast network of internal espionage and coercion, the militarization of society, the vicious use of government-organized mobs to assault dissidents — all are chilling auguries of the brutal future that the Sandinistas have in store for the people of Nicaragua. A fighting chance to spare themselves that future is at least as much in their interests as the ouster of the Sandinistas is in ours.

NICARAGUA: A THREAT
TO OUR SECURITY?

NO MILITARY THREAT TO U.S.

John Buell and Matthew Rothschild

John Buell and Matthew Rothschild are associate editors of
The Progressive magazine. They discuss the economic and
psychological concerns that the Sandinista revolution raises
for the United States.

Points to Consider

1. How do revolutions in poor nations threaten U.S.
   economic interests?
2. What threats do the Sandinistas pose for U.S. corporate
   interests in Central America?
3. Why would a moral foreign policy lower U.S. living
   standards?
4. What is threatening about contemporary economic
   growth?

If we are to conduct a moral foreign policy, we will have to learn as a people to live on a more modest scale.

President Reagan asserts that the revolution in Nicaragua might spread across Central America, and he is right. He claims that the Sandinistas threaten the interests of the United States; again, he is right.

The Threat of Revolution

It's time to grab the bull by the horns. Yes, the Sandinistas may hasten the advent or triumph of revolutions in El Salvador, Guatemala, Honduras, Panama, and even Mexico. Yes, American companies and American consumers may suffer as result. That's the price we should be prepared to pay for a moral foreign policy.

Two centuries ago, Alexis de Tocqueville saw that the American and French revolutions would spur similar upheavals in other nations. He understood that the ideology of freedom and the example of greater economic and political equality were bound to appeal to peoples all over the world. Tocqueville recognized that hope, not misery, was the wellspring of radical change. Today, the Sandinistas provide the hope.

With the overthrow of Anastasio Somoza in 1979, the Sandinistas showed that the old order was not immutable. By instituting real land reform, successful literacy drives, and a massive public health program, they have persuaded others in the region that positive change is possible.

"We export ideas, ideas of change and renovation," said Sergio Ramirez Mercado, a member of the Sandinista Junta, in a 1983 speech. "How can one prevent a peasant in another Central American country from hearing, from finding out, from realizing that in Nicaragua land is given to other poor and barefoot peasants like him? How can you avoid his realizing that here children—not his children—are being vaccinated while his children still die of gastroenteritis and polio?"

Revolutions spread, but not in the way Ronald Reagan imagines.

Sandinista Threat

To what extent does the Sandinista revolution threaten U.S. interests?

It does not, by any stretch of paranoid imagination, threaten the "national security" of the United States. If all of Central America, including Mexico, were to undergo leftist revolutions, this country would face no military threat. The Pentagon would not topple.

Constant American Meddling

We had descended upon Nicaragua with a swarm of armed marines, of American officials, of American experts, and colonial carpet-baggers, to impose American theories of government and democracy by force (a procedure contrary to these very theories). There were either some hare-brained utopians in the State Department or somebody was playing blindman's bluff with the American public . . .

Nicaragua at the time of my visit, after eighteen years of almost constant American meddling, much of which was attended by American financial, military and political control and by the employment of high-priced experts, was in a truly miserable condition . . .

It is significant that when I was there, its cities were dilapidated, its public buildings run down and dirty; that it had few miles of railway and roads . . .

The post-office service, and in fact nearly every public service, was a joke. Nicaragua, under our paternal tutelage for so many years, had become the most backward and miserable of all Central American Republics.

Carleton Beals reporting from Nicaragua in 1931 on Sandino's fight against the U.S. military occupation.

So what's all the fuss?

The fuss is economic—and psychological.

U.S. corporations have more than $10 billion invested in Central America. If leftist governments came to power in all of the region, the corporations might not make as much money as they did before. Their access to cheap labor and raw materials, as well as their ability to negotiate lollipop contracts with Central American oligarchs, might diminish.

American consumers could also be placed at a disadvantage. Central America exports coffee, bananas, and manufactured products to the U.S. market—though it is usually U.S. corporations doing the exporting. If leftist regimes managed to attain power, U.S. consumers of such commodities might have to pay a higher price.

And Mexico accounts for a large share of our oil imports; if it were to become hostile to the United States, oil prices might shoot up and strain our economy. (This is improbable, however, since any Mexican government would need to sell oil to the United States at some near-market price; otherwise, Mexico would lose its major trading partner.)

The American Empire

The economic challenge posed by Central America is the economic challenge posed by the Third World. In the glory days of the American empire, from World War II to the late 1960s, we thrived on bargain-basement prices for raw materials, oppressively low foreign wages, and golden investment opportunities in the Third World. To no small degree, these windfalls accounted for the unprecedented U.S. standard of living in this period. But as Third World countries, most notably those in the oil cartel, have begun pursuing more nationalistic economic policies, the United States has had more difficulty asserting its political and economic might. This accounts, in part, for the decline in our standard of living.

Americans have grown accustomed to enjoying a vastly disproportionate share of the world's wealth. If we are to conduct a moral foreign policy, we will have to learn as a people to live on a more modest scale.

But the American psyche is pegged to being biggest, best, richest, and strongest. Just listen to the rhetoric of our politicians, or behold the chauvinistic spectacle that was the Olympics. When a Third World nation—whether it be Cuba, Vietnam, Iran, or Nicaragua—spurns our way of doing things, our egos ache even more than our pocketsbooks. We can't stand to be, in Richard Nixon's memorable phrase, a pitiful, helpless giant.

In this sense, too, Nicaragua poses a threat. It calls into question the way our own society is run, and it repudiates our type of economic system and representative government. In so doing, it assaults our self-image, our notion of identity.

Intervention and War

The economic and psychological imperatives of the American empire propel us inexorably toward intervention and war. They also direct us down a wasteful and destructive path of existence. We devote precious time, energy, and human resources to develop technologies that perpetuate our power. And in the process, we become enslaved.

The Guardian

Though many liberals and leftists denounce the "irrationality" of the arms race, that race is rational in the sense that the ever-expanding exploitation of the Earth's resources and people requires the ceaseless development of arms technology.

Contemporary economic growth is similarly threatening, both on the level of the individual and on the level of society. To put more red meat on every table, we constantly expand food production through use of nitrogen fertilizers which, in turn, pollute rivers, erode farm lands, and deplete resources. And the meat on our tables induces heart attacks and cancer.

Our modern industrial-military society resembles nothing so much as a dog chasing its own tail. The harder it runs, the harder it must strive to catch up.

In his attempt to enslave, the master himself has become locked into a set of interests and commitments that keep him from attaining his full humanity. U.S. policy toward Nicaragua is but the latest installment of the American tragedy.

23 NICARAGUA: A THREAT TO OUR SECURITY?

DANGER TO OUR BORDERS

Phyllis Schlafly

Phyllis Schlafly is the author and publisher of The Phyllis Schlafly Report *and a prominent conservative spokeswoman on national and international issues.*

Points to Consider

1. What repressive tactics have the Sandinistas used in Nicaragua?
2. What happened to the Miskito Indians?
3. How is the military buildup in Nicaragua described?
4. What refugee problems could arise for Americans if communism triumphs in Central America?

"U.S. Stakes in Central America," *The Phyllis Schlafly Report*, August, 1985, pp. 1-3.

The legal obligations of our President under the Monroe Doctrine, and the Organization of American States and the Rio Grande Treaties, make it the duty of our President to take action against the aggression in Nicaragua, as we did in Grenada.

When Congress voted in April against President Reagan's request to send $14 million to help the Freedom Fighters in Nicaragua, within hours the Sandinista dictator Daniel Ortega rushed to Moscow to hug Mikhail Gorbachev and receive pledges of Soviet military aid. This embarrassed Congress enough to reverse itself in June and impelled Secretary of State George Shultz to talk about the Communist threat in Central America.

Indeed, there are really Communists in Nicaragua. The Sandinista dictatorship does what Communist dictatorships always do. It created a secret police system to control the people, assisted by Soviet, East German, and Cuban Communists. It punishes freedom of speech, press and assembly by officially-sanctioned harassment, imprisonment or death.

The Sandinistas go after their political opposition with typical Communist brutality. They recently jailed ten members of the Social Christian Party and treated them as the Communists have treated political prisoners in other countries from Russia to Cuba. They are held in small, dark cells and served meals at irregular intervals in order to disorient them. In order to coerce their prisoners into confessing to crimes they did not commit, the Sandinistas arrested the relatives of the prisoner.

Jose Gonzales, a former vice president of the Social Democratic Party, told Pope John Paul II there were about 8,000 political prisoners in 1981, and that they were the victims of repression and torture. Gonzales finally left Nicaragua and now lives in exile.

161

Forced Relocations

Under a "scorched earth" policy copied from Cambodia, the Sandinistas have ordered and are carrying out the forced relocation of tens of thousands of peasants. Some 20,000 peasants have been moved from their homes to relocation camps, and the Sandinistas admit this resettlement project involves 65,000 people. Peasants and journalists tell of entire villages, homes, stores, and churches being burnt to the ground. They tell of animals slaughtered, crops and villages burned.

The cutting edge of the Sandinistas' atrocities is their treatment of the Miskito Indians. The Miskitos supported the Sandinistas against the previous ruler, Somoza, but that didn't save them from becoming victims of Communist brutality after they resisted Marxist indoctrination.

The Miskitos were then labelled "bourgeois" and "enemies of the people." The Sandinistas began to arrest the Miskito Indian leaders, torture and murder them. Eyewitnesses have told about massacres, Indians buried alive, 10,000 force-marched to relocation camps, their villages burned down, bombed and shelled. Tens of thousands of Miskitos have fled the Nicaragua where they've lived for more than a thousand years.

Liberal friends of the Sandinistas have propagated the myth that they enjoy popular support in Nicaragua. The Sandinistas sustain their support by such methods as confiscating ration cards for non-attendance at Sandinista meetings. Talk of inflation is branded a counterrevolutionary plot.

One would think that the Sandinistas would have a big job trying to improve conditions in Nicaragua. But like typical Communists, they are intensely engaged in spreading their Communist revolution beyond their borders. The Sandinistas provide arms, training, and a headquarters to the Communist guerrillas who are attempting to overthrow the democratically-elected Duarte government of El Salvador. The Sandinistas also support anti-democratic movements in Honduras, Costa Rica, and Guatemala.

In Southeast Asia, the "falling dominoes" theory became a bitter reality. After the fall of South Vietnam, Laos and Cambodia fell, too. That's the Nicaragua/Vietnam parallel.

More than a quarter million refugees have already fled

Nicaragua since the Sandinistas took control. Unless the Freedom Fighters take back their country from the Communists, Nicaragua will send us more millions of refugees, and the "falling dominoes" in Central America will massively escalate the number. The refugees from Southeast Asia, and even from Cuba, had to come by boat. But the refugees from Central America can just walk north across the Rio Grande.

Threats from Nicaragua

Since Congressional committees in recent years seldom provide a forum for witnesses with expertise on the subject of internal security, some private organizations have tried to fill the gap. A group of military and intelligence experts collaborating under the name "National Committee to Restore Internal Security" has published the transcript of a hearing it held in the Senate Hart Office Building on threats to the United States from Nicaragua.

The witnesses told how Nicaragua has not only become a base for an extraordinary and dramatic buildup of military weapons and equipment, but has also become a major part of the international drug system. The Sandinistas are replacing Columbia as a leading processor of cocaine and, with the help of the Cuban naval escorts, are moving enormous amounts of cocaine into the United States.

The accelerated military buildup in Nicaragua is far more extensive and dramatic than was the buildup rate in Cuba. It is probably faster than has ever occurred in a peacetime situation anywhere in the world.

Seek Actions, Not Words

Experience has taught that we must seek actions, not words, from Nicaragua—action to sever military and security ties to Cuba and the Soviet bloc; action to end all support for guerrilla violence and terrorism in Central America.

U.S. Department of State, May 2, 1984

Refugees from Communism

History teaches us that, when the Communists take over any country, the result is an immediate, massive exodus, and usually a continuing flow of refugees (depending on the efficiency of the barbed wire fences, mine fields, and border guards). The 30-year, world-wide experience is that 10% of the population emigrates as refugees any time the Communists take over a country.

The American people need to face up to the horrendous prospects of what can happen at our door-step in Latin America. If El Salvador is taken over by the Communists, 10% of its population of 4,700,000, or 470,000 people, would become refugees and walk north.

Here are the 10%-of-population figures in the other countries in Central America: Costa Rica 240,000, Guatemala 750,000, Honduras 410,000, Nicaragua 260,000, and Panama 200,000. If there ever was a part of the world where we should guard against a "falling dominoes" effect, it is Central America.

It would be ridiculous to think that our neighbor to the south, Mexico, would or could absorb these refugees. Mexico already has tremendous unemployment and is in debt up to its ears. If Central America falls, Mexico could fall, too, and 10% of its population of 69,400,000 (that means 6,940,000 refugees) would walk north in addition to the two million from Central America.

Could we close our borders to neighbors who face certain persecution from new Communist dictators subsidized by Moscow? Could we accept the costs of this new influx of refugees — costs in social-program dollars and in domestic conflicts? How would we face the blurring of the difference between immigrants and refugees? If it were a simple matter of residence preference, much of the rest of the world would probably want to come to the United States.

NICARAGUA: A THREAT TO OUR SECURITY?

MARXISM AND THE SANDINISTAS: THE POINT

Ron Perrin

Ron Perrin is a professor of political theory at the University of Montana in Missoula, Montana. He is working on a new book on the "Reconstruction of Democratic Theory."

Points to Consider

1. What revolutions did the U.S. oppose?
2. Why does the Nicaraguan revolution threaten American capitalism?
3. How do U.S. corporate interests profit from poverty and oppression in poor nations?
4. What is revolutionary Marxism?
5. How has Marxism been revised?

Ron Perrin, "Yes, But Is It Marxism?" *National Catholic Reporter,* March 29, 1984, pp. 7, 8. Reprinted by permission, National Catholic Reporter, PO Box 281, Kansas City, Missouri 64141.

There is a chain of production and distribution that runs from the sweat shops of Hong Kong to the K-marts of America's suburbs.

Hardly a week goes by before Ronald Reagan is moved once again to condemn the "Sandinista thugs" who govern Nicaragua. At various times Reagan has portrayed the Sandinista movement as one of the most vicious regimes in the world today, one of the most vicious regimes of all time, or simply the source of all the difficulties that the U.S. government has in Central America.

Anyone who has been awake the past few years will know that Reagan has a host of candidates to choose from in awarding the Sandinistas his "thugs of the decade" prize. Dictatorships, violations of human rights and grievous neglect of basic physical needs abound: from Chile to Cambodia, from South Africa to El Salvador. Why, then, even if they were true, this drumbeat of charges against the government of Nicaragua? And why the openly admitted attempt to overthrow that government, a government that has recently held the first democratic elections in the memory of any living Nicaraguan?

The first, and simplest, answer is that if the United States did *not* oppose the Nicaraguan revolution, a historical precedent would be established. A brief historical survey serves to indicate just how significant that precedent would be.

— In 1918 the United States, with Great Britain and France, mounted an expeditionary force to aid the supporters of the deposed czarist regime in Russia. The "enemy" was the newly established government of Nikolai Lenin and his Bolshevik party, the first self-proclaimed Marxist regime in history.

— Between 1945 and 1948 the United States supported the right-wing government of Chiang Kai-shek against the Communist party and army of Mao Tse-tung. When Mao's Marxist revolution succeeded in gaining power, the United States recognized only the exiled government of Chiang as the legitimate representative of the Chinese people.

— In 1953 the CIA engineered the ouster of Premier Mossadegh in Iran, paving the way for the authoritarian

166

regime of the shah of Iran. Mossadegh had been the leader of a National Front movement whose policies included the nationalization of the oil industry. The shah dutifully allowed a consortium of American, French and Dutch companies to operate Iran's oil facilities.

— In 1954 the United States aided in the overthrow of the Jacobo Arbenz government in Guatemala. That government, Marxist in principle but not in its official proclamations, had expropriated the large agricultural estates in Guatemala. The most prominent among them were the land holdings of the United Fruit Co. of North America.

— In 1973 the CIA supported and aided in the overthrow of the Salvador Allende government in Chile. Allende was an avowed Marxist who came to power in a democratic election. His policies included the nationalization of industrial properties owned by U.S. firms and initiation of a land reform program.

— From 1961 to 1973 the United States was directly involved in a war against communism in Southeast Asia. Once more, the immediate issues were land reform and the ouster of Western economic interests.

One could cite the attempted overthrow and continuing boycott of Cuba, the attempted assassinations of Fidel Castro or the support of anticommunist dictatorships around the world, wherever there is a real or perceived threat of Marxism. The point, however, is made: The Sandinistas have incurred the wrath and militant opposition of the Reagan

Reagan Is Lying

Those who have gone to find out the truth for themselves have returned from Nicaragua with a picture very different from the distorted image propagated by this administration. The official falsehood has become a great conspiracy of lies designed to confuse the American public and to provide the rationale for more direct U.S. military intervention in Nicaragua.

Sojourners, August, 1984

administration because they represent the latest and nearest manifestation of revolutionary Marxism.

Revolutionary Marxism

What, then, is revolutionary Marxism and how does it pose a threat to the national interests of the United States?

The growth of the United States into a global power was a direct consequence of the international expansion of its capitalist economy. A basic principle of such an economy is that material development is best achieved when capital investment is free to discover and develop the cheapest sources of raw material and labor. This condition is best served when the people who provide that raw material and labor are rigidly controlled by a minority of their people who profit enormously by the arrangement. In other words, the penetration of the U.S. economy into the less-developed regions of the world has been greatly enhanced where the populations of those regions remain economically impoverished and politically unorganized.

The economic and political principles of Marxism run directly counter to these circumstances. One common feature in all the episodes cited above was the attempt to replace private or corporate control of the economy with some form of social ownership. This reflects the Marxist insistence that economic development is best achieved when a nation's resources are collectively controlled and developed. The vehicle through which this is to be accomplished is a national or Communist party that must be strong and militant enough to meet the capitalist nations on their own terms. The establishment of this communist power necessarily involves the revolutionary overthrow of the wealthy minorities who have directed the nation's economy to their own advantage.

When Karl Marx developed his theory, he had in mind the economies of the industrialized nations of Western Europe and North America. There, he thought, society would become increasingly polarized between a minority of wealthy capitalists and a majority of impoverished workers. Contrary to this prediction, the majority of the populations in the industrialized West have, until now, enjoyed a rather high standard of living.

168

"We've arrived at the border with Nicaragua. I can confirm that they are threatening us something awful and, I think, are already sapping us!"

Drawing by Vsevolod ARSENYEV

But this general state of affluence and the political stability it affords have been purchased at the expense of the Third World. There is a chain of production and distribution that runs from the sweat shops of Hong Kong to the K-marts of America's suburbs. It is the same chain that ran from the coffee fields of Nicaragua to the percolators in America's kitchens. One does not have to be a Marxist to know that if the people at the far end of that chain receive more, then the people at this end will receive less. *Providing, that is, that the same degree of profits is extracted at every link along that chain.* And the bottom line of the American economy is profit.

This, then, is the way U.S. interests are threatened by any political development in the Third World that promises fundamentally to improve living conditions; particularly the living conditions of the peasants, who still comprise more than two-thirds of the world's laboring population.

If you are sitting where Reagan is sitting, it is not difficult to perceive of Marxism or communism as a monolithic movement. From the perspective of U.S. corporate interests, the effects of Marxist revolutions, wherever they occur, are the same: less economic control, less political power, less profit. What is more, the cause of these revolutions — an interlocking system of poverty, illiteracy and oppression — is the same.

Marxist Revisions

However, the agent and context of radical economic and social change are not, and need not be, the same. For one, the Soviet Union has proved incapable of directing the affairs of an international network of Communist parties. Even in the bordering states of Eastern Europe those parties are increasingly displaying a will of their own.

Far more important is the fact that — for better or worse — Marxist revolutions tend to follow the contours of the prevailing culture and traditions. This has been the case ever since Joseph Stalin's policies came to embody the superstition, paranoia and brutality that were so typical of the czarist regimes that preceded him. What is more, these policies were fueled by the tendency of the allied expedition against the Bolsheviks to rekindle Russian memories of earlier invasions by the West.

The result was the first revision in Marx's theory of revolution. For Marx's claim that the communist revolution must be the united task of workers throughout the industrialized world, Stalin substituted the premise that communism could be established under the authority of a highly centralized party that would literally force the Soviet Union into the industrial age.

The influence that tradition exerts upon any attempt radically to alter current economic, social and political arrangements is just as evident in the history of the Chinese revolution. There the circumstances of China's agrarian economy and a long-standing pattern of social involvement by intellectuals have helped to accomplish a revision of Marx's revolutionary theory that is every bit as significant as Stalin's concept of "Socialism in One Country."

It was the leadership of the Chinese revolution that made the practice of land reform a basic tenet of Marxist revolutionary practice. Mao correctly judged that the basic cause of poverty and economic exploitation in China lay with the domination of the peasantry by the landlords. Accordingly, Mao substituted the peasants for the industrial workers as the class whose needs and energies could best serve the transformation of Chinese society into a communist state.

Echoes of prerevolutionary China were also evident in Mao's repeated insistence that the Red army and the Communist party must subordinate their interests to the interests of the Chinese masses. This concern is wholly consistent with the many revivals of Confucianism in the Chinese past, particularly the emphasis in Confucianism upon ethical precepts that enjoin its followers to devote themselves to the proper care and management of society.

This Hemisphere

If we turn our attention to the development of revolutionary Marxism in this hemisphere, the picture changes somewhat but the same continuity of pre- and post-revolutionary themes prevails. In Cuba, for example, Castro's struggle against the Fulgencio Batista dictatorship was waged against the advice and support of the Cuban Communist party. Castro drew his inspiration from the saga of Jose Marti, the father of Cuba's independence from Spanish rule, rather than from the theory of Marx. Only after the Cuban

revolution consolidated its power did Castro and Che
Guevara turn to the study of Marxism in their search for
some understanding of Cuba's long history of economic
dependence upon the United States. And, here again, the
most radical intentions were forced to make their compromise with traditional practice.

Castro and Guevara reasoned that as long as Cuba remained a one-crop economy the revolution could be held hostage
to the dictates of the world market in sugar. Therefore, they
concluded, economic as well as political independence
could be furthered by the diversification of the economy into
the production of cattle, manufactured goods and so on.
Whatever the theoretical merits of this argument, the practical consequences were very nearly disastrous as the gross
national product plummeted. Now, as before, 85 percent of
the value of Cuba's exports stems from the market in sugar
and its by-products.

Back to Nicaragua

Which brings us back to Nicaragua. Whatever else
Nicaragua has been and is, it is Catholic. The Sandinistas
apparently know, as Castro seems to know and the Polish
Communist party clearly knows, that the legitimacy of their
governance depends upon an accommodation with the
church. What I find exceptional in the Nicaraguan instance
is that the knowledge flows in both directions.

There, a good part of the clergy are aware that their
legitimacy, as well, is dependent upon insuring that the
revolution be held to its promises. This clergy cannot remain
indifferent to the hopes that have been aroused in the people without losing those people — in body and/or in soul —
to what would then become a communist theocracy.

This is the context within which a Catholic can call herself
or himself a Marxist. And, not incidentally, the context within
which a Marxist can call himself or herself a Christian. If the
Nicaraguan revolution is to be a *human* event, rather than
merely a political or economic event, the Sandinistas will
have to embrace the spiritual concerns of the church; and
the ministry of the Nicaraguan clergy will have to be leaven-
ed by the materialistic concerns of Marxism. Should this
occur, the Nicaraguan revolution will be noteworthy not only
for its success, but also for having accomplished another
extraordinary revision of revolutionary Marxism.

172

NICARAGUA: A THREAT TO OUR SECURITY?

MARXISM AND THE SANDINISTAS: THE COUNTERPOINT

John Silber

John Silber is the president of Boston University. He is a prominent national spokesman for conservative ideas and causes.

Points to Consider

1. What are the three myths regarding U.S. policy toward Central America?
2. Why are the Sandinistas defined as Marxists?
3. Why should aid be given to the Contras?
4. What mistake did the democracies make in the 1930's?

Excerpted from a statement by John Silber in testimony before the House Committee on Foreign Affairs, April 16, 1985.

If the regime in Managua does not yet perfectly resemble that in Havana or Moscow, it is only because, for reasons to which I will return, it has not yet managed to consolidate its control.

The island of Cuba has become a massive Soviet forward base from which revolution is exported to Central America. It is not my purpose to trace the steps by which this came to be but to ask whether the United States is prepared to tolerate in our hemisphere the consolidation of a second Soviet satellite.

In my opinion, our country is now confronted with problems less sensational but no less dangerous than those that President Kennedy faced and solved, however temporarily.

Discussions of U.S. Policy are Developed by Historical Myth

All discussions of U.S. policy in Central America are bedeviled by historical myth. This is especially true of our policies toward Nicaragua. There are three controlling myths: The first is that the Sandinistas were incipient democrats whom an unkind United States drove into the arms of Cuba and the Soviet Union, and who would yet create a democratic Nicaragua if we only gave them time and approached them diplomatically. No one who has read the pronouncements of the present Sandinista leadership before it took power could fall victim to this delusion. The Sandinistas described themselves as Marxist-Leninists long before 1979, and the subsequent statement by the Sandinista leaders once in power only confirmed this.

It is crucial to understand, moreover, that "Marxism-Leninism" is neither a buzzword nor epithet but the name of a precisely defined political system whose nature has been revealed in nearly 70 years of unvarying practice. No Marxist-Leninist regime has ever submitted itself to the discipline of free elections, not to the discipline of a free press, nor of

174

free trade unions. Such regimes have permitted no genuine competitors for political power. Indeed, they have not even tolerated unauthorized private organizations.

This brief recapitulation of the obvious enables us to understand and predict the behavior of the Sandinista regime. It began, like most such regimes with the seizure of power, first from the tyrants of the older order, and then from the democrats who had helped drive them out. It continued with the suppression of free speech and free media, curbs on free trade unions and private enterprise, and restrictions on the free exercise of religion. No Leninist regime has ever voluntarily moderated such behavior. The precedent, on the contrary, is for its intensification until the Sandinistas have throttled the last remains of free institutions in Nicaragua. If the regime in Managua does not yet perfectly resemble that in Havana or Moscow, it is only because, for reasons to which I will return, it has not yet managed to consolidate its control.

All historical experience suggests that hopes of a merely diplomatic solution to the crisis posed by the Sandinistas are almost certain to be disappointed. The only solution likely to come from diplomacy when it is unsupported by intensive pressure is the sort that was reached in Munich in 1938. Diplomacy is a complement to, not a substitute for, the measured application of geostrategic pressure.

The myth that the Sandinistas are misunderstood democrats, as well as others that I will be discussing, did

Suppression of Dissent

The most decisive strides of the Sandinistas toward the Soviets and toward the suppression of dissent took place when the Carter administration was the main international provider of funds to the Sandinistas and when most domestic Nicaraguan sectors and most Western democratic nations were on good terms with them.

Humberto Belli, *Imprimis,* **June, 1984**

not just grow. They have been hyped through the latest marketing techniques by among others, a Washington and New York-based p.r. firm working on behalf of the Sandinista leadership, Fenton Communications, Inc., Newsletter, which in its newsletter opposes the funding of the Contras in Nicaragua and engages in this effort to control public opinion in America.

The second myth is that military and political forces now opposing the Sandinistas are dominated by former Somocistas, members of the Somoza regime fighting to restore the old order. This argument conveniently overlooks the role that was played in the struggle against Somoza by the major figures now fighting for democracy against the Sandinistas. One of these leaders, Eden Pastora, a hero of the Sandinista forces before the revolution, was described by Somoza himself in his memoirs as "a Communist terrorist." Others, such as Arturo Cruz and Violeta Chamorro, were members of the revolutionary junta before being forced out by the Sandinistas. Many others, including Alfonso Robelo, Adolfo Calero, and Alfredo Cesar, had actively opposed Somoza, and had been in his jails. . .

A third myth is that armed revolution led by the extreme left will bring democracy to Central America. The fact is that armed revolution has brought despotism, not democracy, to Nicaragua. In El Salvador, by contrast, Jose Napoleon Duarte's courageous democratic leadership, backed politically, militarily, and economically by the United States, has produced an increasingly broad-based and democratic government despite the pressures and chaos imposed by a Marxist-Leninist insurgency.

We must recognize that El Salvador and Nicaragua pose instructive opposites: El Salvador is an imperfect democratic government. Its failures in human rights are most accurately described as its inability to embody its own principles, while it resists overthrow by totalitarians. Nicaragua is a totalitarian government. Its failures in human rights are most accurately described as the fulfillment of its own principles, while it resists overthrow by the forces of democracy. In El Salvador, we have a government whose inadequate guarantees of human rights demonstrate its present inability to live up to its ideals; in Nicaragua, the inadequacy is much more serious. It reveals the program of a government fully

By David Seavey, USA TODAY

living up to its ideals, under which the very concept of human rights independent of the state is meaningless.

Nothing is more reasonable, therefore, than that the United States should support both democracy in El Salvador by aiding a freely elected government against its armed enemies, and democracy in Nicaragua, by aiding the democratic opponents of the regime. I am aware that many patriotic Americans, some of them distinguished members of this subcommittee, oppose aid to the Nicaraguan rebels and do so on highly principled grounds. I should like to pose, for these and other Americans, several questions. If we should not be aiding the Nicaraguan rebels now, at what point, if any, should we aid them? Those who would answer "never," whether they know it or not, are consigning the people of Nicaragua to an enduring Leninist despotism. If the Congress refuses to support those fighting for democracy in Nicaragua, the Sandinistas will conclude that they have succeeded in neutralizing the United States. We can then expect an immediate consolidation of the regime. Let us be clear what this consolidation will mean: The final suppression of free speech, free press, free trade unions, free religion, and the utter abolition of any vestige of pluralism in Nicaraguan society. It would certainly mean a vastly increased persecution of the Miskito Indians.

To those who would answer, "We will support democracy in Nicaragua eventually, but not now." I would ask, "when?" When the Sandinistas finally snuff out the flickering light of La Prensa? When they abolish the last free trade union? When they abolish all political parties but their own? I have said "when" rather than "if" because all of these actions are inevitable.

There are other contingencies to which if applies. Would one favor support for the rebels if the Sandinistas acquire MIG fighters or more attack helicopters? If they step up their support of the rebels in El Salvador? If they begin exporting revolution to Honduras, Guatemala, or Costa Rica? If they invade any of these countries? At this point, of course, the question of aid to the freedom fighters will be moot, for they will long since have been crushed. The question will be whether one favors the survival of freedom and democracy in Central America, for by that time, the Cuban and Soviet forces will pose a serious and direct threat to Mexico and to the United States.

The price of containing Soviet adventurism in the Americas will never be as cheap, in dollars and in blood, as it is today. Better by far to aid the so-called "Contras" today than to send in the marines later. Absent pressures of the type and intensity brought to bear by the democratic rebels, the Sandinista leadership will have no reason to negotiate a democratic outcome.

It is crucial in this to distinguish between El Salvador, where the overwhelming majority of those in authority are committed to democracy, and the situation in Nicaragua. Like all Leninists, the Sandinistas proclaim the goals of freedom and abundance. But like all Leninists, they will fasten upon the Nicaraguan people a system opposed to

178

freedom and incapable of producing abundance. . .

The price Americans are now asked to pay for ending the Soviet-Cuban adventure in Nicaragua is very small. But with each month it will rise. The United States, like Britain and France, will eventually pay the greatly escalated price that inaction will make inexorable. The Congress still has a chance to keep the price low by its continued support of the Nicaraguan rebels.

In aiding the Contras, the United States has the opportunity to avoid the errors of the democracies in the late 1930's. Had the French, for example, sent no more than a division into Germany when Hitler remilitarized the Rhineland, he would have been forced into a humiliating withdrawal that would probably have precipitated his removal from power. Had Chamberlain not gone to Munich, a well-advanced plot by the German high command to remove Hitler would have been put into effect and almost certainly succeeded. But the allies preferred to believe that Hitler would respond to diplomacy devoid of power—and, acting on this illusion, they left no alternative to war. Their intentions were admirable: to avoid a repetition of the carnage of the First World War. In the end, however, their admirable intentions did not prevent the carnage. And the lesson lives on.

RECOGNIZING AUTHOR'S POINT OF VIEW

This activity may be used as an individualized study guide for students in libraries and resource centers or as a discussion catalyst in small group and classroom discussions.

Many readers are unaware that written material usually expresses an opinion or bias. The capacity to recognize an author's point of view is an essential reading skill. The skill to read with insight and understanding involves the ability to detect different kinds of opinions or bias. Sex bias, race bias, ethnocentric bias, political bias and religious bias are five basic kinds of opinions expressed in editorials and all literature that attempts to persuade. They are briefly defined in the glossary below.

5 Kinds of Editorial Opinion or Bias

sex bias— the expression of dislike for and/or feeling of superiority over the opposite sex or a particular sexual minority

race bias— the expression of dislike for and/or feeling of superiority over a racial group

*ethnocentric bias—the expression of a belief that one's own group, race, religion, culture or nation is superior. Ethnocentric persons judge others by their own standards and values.

*political bias—the expression of political opinions and attitudes about domestic or foreign affairs

*religious bias—the expression of a religious belief or attitude

Guidelines

1. Locate three examples of political opinion or bias in the readings from chapter 5.

2. Locate five sentences that provide examples of any kind of editorial opinion or bias from the readings in chapter 5.

3. Write down each of the above sentences and determine what kind of bias each sentence represents. Is it **sex bias, race bias, ethnocentric bias, political bias or religious bias?**

4. Make up one sentence statements that would be an example of each of the following: **sex bias, race bias, ethnocentric bias, political bias** and **religious bias.**

5. See if you can locate five sentences that are factual statements from the readings in chapter five.

Summarize author's point of view in one sentence for each of the following opinions:

Reading 20 _____

_____

_____

Reading 21 _____

_____

_____

Reading 22 _____

_____

_____

Reading 23 _____

_____

_____

Reading 24 _____

_____

_____

Reading 25 _____

_____

_____

NICARAGUA:
Selected References

Araujo, Richard. *The Sandinista War on Human Rights.* Washington, Heritage Foundation, 1983. 7 p. (Backgrounder no. 277)

Belli, Humberto. "The Church in Nicaragua: Under Attack from Within and Without." *Religion in Communist Lands,* v. 12, spring 1984: 42-54.

Booth, John A. *The End and the Beginning: The Nicaraguan Revolution.* Boulder, Colo., Westview Press, 1982. 279 p. (Westview special studies on Latin America and the Caribbean)

Chamorro Barrio, Carlos Fernando. "Nicaragua: The Military Front and the Political." *New Times* (Moscow), no. 22, May 1984: 10-11.

Crawley, Eduardo. *Nicaragua in Perspective.* Rev. ed. New York, St. Martin's Press, 1984. 208 p.

Duncan, W. Raymond. "Soviet Interests in Latin America." *Journal of American Studies and World Affairs, v. 26, May 1984: 163-198.*

Gershman, Carl. "Soviet Power in Central America and the Caribbean: The Growing Threat to American Security." *AEI Foreign Policy and Defense Review,* v. 5, no. 1, 1984: 37-46.

Human Rights in Nicaragua. New York, Americas Watch Committee, 1984. 51 p.

Inter-American Commission on Human Rights. *Report on the Situation of Human Rights in the Republic of Nicaragua.* Washington, General Secretariat, Organization of American States, 1981. 171 p. (DEA/Ser. L/V/II.53, doc. 25, 30 June 1981, original: Spanish)

Lappe, Frances Moore, and Joseph Collins. *Now We Can Speak: A Journey through the New Nicaragua.* San Francisco, Institute for Food and Development Policy, c1982. 127 p.

Luers, William H. "The Soviets and Latin America: A Three Decade U.S. Policy Tangle." *Washington Quarterly,* v. 7, winter 1984: 3-32.

Nicaragua: A Country Study. Edited by James D. Rudolph. 2nd ed. Washington, Foreign Area Studies, the American University, for sale by the Supt. of Docs., G.P.O, 1982. 278 p.

Nicaragua in Revolution. Edited by Thomas W. Walker. New York, Praeger, 1982. 410 p.

The Nicaragua Reader: Documents of a Revolution Under Fire. Edited by Peter Rosset and John Vandermeer. New York, Grove Press, 1983. 359 p.

Radosh, Ronald. "Darkening Nicaragua." *New Republic,* v. 189, Oct. 24, 1983: 7-12.

Reed, Roger. *Nicaraguan Military Operations and Covert Activities in Latin America.* Washington, Council for Inter-American Security, 1982. 34 p.

Rosenberg, Mark B. "Nicaragua and Honduras: Toward Garrison States." *Current History,* v. 83, Feb. 1984: 59-62, 87.

United Nations. Security Council. *Military and Paramilitary Activities in and Against Nicaragua.* New York, United Nations, 1984. 43 p. (United Nations. Document S/16564)

U.S. Policy and Programs

Araujo, Richard. *The Nicaraguan Connection: A Threat to Central America.* Washington, Heritage Foundation, 1982. 20 p.

Cruz, Arturo J. "Nicaragua: The Sandinista Regime at a Watershed." *Strategic Review,* v. 12, spring 1984: 11-23.

Gleijeses, Piero. "Resist Romanticism." *Foreign Policy,* no. 54, spring 1984: 122-138.

Gutman, Roy. "America's Diplomatic Charade." *Foreign Policy,* no. 56, fall 1984: 3-23.

Hutchinson, John. "Here We Come? Here We Go?" *National Review,* v. 36, Feb. 24, 1984: 28-31, 36, 38.

Nicaragua's Military Build-up and Support for Central American Subversion: Background Paper. Washington, 1984. 37 p. Released by the Department of State and Department of Defense.

Sanchez, Nestor D. "Revolutionary Change and the Nicaraguan People." *Strategic Review,* v. 12, summer 1984: 17-22.

Tierney, John J., Jr. *Somozas and Sandinistas: The U.S. and Nicaragua in the Twentieth Century.* Washington, Council for Inter-American Security, c1982. 95 p.

Central America

Background

The Americas at a Crossroads: Report of the InterAmerican Dialogue. Washington, Smithsonian Institution, Wilson Center, 1983. 63 p.

Bulmer-Thomas, V. "Crisis in Central America—Economic Roots and Historical Dimensions." *World Today,* v. 39, Sept. 1984: 328-335.

Caribbean and Central American Databook. 3rd ed. Washington, Caribbean/Central American Action, 1984. 387 p.

"Central America and the Caribbean." *Journal of Latin American Studies,* v. 15, Nov. 1983: whole issue.

Central America: Crisis and Adaptation, edited by Steve C. Ropp and James A. Morris. Albuquerque, University of New Mexico Press, 1984. 311 p.

Central America in Crisis. Rev. ed. Washington, Washington Institute for Values in Public Policy, 1983. 277 p.

Communism in Central America and the Caribbean. Edited by Robert Wesson. Stanford, Calif., Hoover Institution Press, c1982. 177 p. (Hoover international studies)

Ferris, Elizabeth G. "The Politics of Asylum: Mexico and the Central American Refugees." *Journal of InterAmerican Studies and World Affairs,* v. 26, Aug. 1984: 357-384.

"Latin America, 1984." *Current History,* v. 83, Feb. 1984: whole issue.

Leiken, Robert S. *Soviet Strategy in Latin America.* [New York] Praeger [1982] 124 p. (Washington papers, v. 10, no. 93)

Rift and Revolution: The Central American Imbroglio. Washington, American Enterprise Institute for Public Policy Research, c1984. 392 p. (AEI studies, 394)

Woodward, Ralph Lee, Jr. "The Rise and Decline of Liberalism in Central America." *Journal of InterAmerican Studies and World Affairs,* v. 26, Aug. 1984: 291-312.

U.S. Policy and Programs

"Central America." *Nation,* v. 238, Jan. 28, 1984: whole issue.

Central America: Anatomy of Conflict. Edited by Robert S. Leiken. New York, Pergamon Press, c1984. 351 p.

Changing Course: Blueprint for Peace in Central America and the Caribbean. Prepared by Policy Alternatives for the Caribbean and Central America. Washington, Institute for Policy Studies, 1984. 112 p.

Crisis and Opportunity: U.S. Policy in Central America and the Caribbean: Thirty Essays by Statesman, Scholars, Religious Leaders, and Journalists. Edited by Mark Falcoff and Robert Royal. Washington, Ethics and Public Policy Center, 1984. 491 p.

"Disposition of U.S. Forces in Central America." In Extension of remarks of Lee H. Hamilton. *Congressional Record* [daily ed.], v. 130, May 16, 1984: E2200-E2202.

From Gunboats to Diplomacy: New U.S. Policies for Latin America. Edited by Richard Newfarmer. Baltimore, Johns Hopkins University Press, c1984. 254 p.

LaFeber, Walter. "The Reagan Administration and Revolutions in Central America." *Political Science Quarterly,* v. 99, spring 1984: 1-25.

LeoGrande, William M. "Through the Looking Glass: The Kiss Report on Central America." *World Policy Journal,* v. 1, winter 1984: 251-284.

Luers, William H. "The Soviets and Latin America: A Three Decade U.S. Policy Tangle." *Washington Quarterly,* v. 7, winter 1984: 3-32.

Moorer, Thomas H., and Georges A. Fauriol. *Caribbean Basin Security.* New York, Praeger, 1983. 108 p.